READER'S COMMENTS

*"After Bill Eddy gave a statewide seminar to our family court judges in 2005, I received the highest ratings ever on our feedback forms. His knowledge and examples as an experienced lawyer and therapist were extremely helpful to them. He went beyond just explaining the problem (as many speakers do) and offered many specific tools to manage these parties. **Managing High Conflict People in Court** provides these tools in a nutshell."*

Megan Hunter, MBA
Vice President, High Conflict Institute
Former Family Law Specialist, Administrative
Office of the Courts, Arizona Supreme Court

"As a frequent trainer of family law judges and attorneys, I find Mr. Eddy's book to be an excellent resource for judges and attorneys. Bill Eddy captures the critical components of Cluster B personality disorders and teaches how they often contribute to the high conflict population."

Philip Stahl, Ph.D.
Author of "Parenting After Divorce"

*"**Managing High Conflict People in Court** is not a dry, academic text, but a succinct, highly pragmatic, and extremely useful tool for Judges and court personnel to understand, and cope with high conflict people in court, thereby having more **orderly, effective,** and **fair** court hearings, for all parties to the dispute."*

Judge Sol Gothard, JD, MSW, ACSW
Fifth Circuit Court of Appeal, LA (ret)

D1563225

NEW WAYS
FOR FAMILIES

Professional Guidebook

NEW WAYS
FOR FAMILIES

By Bill Eddy, LCSW, ESQ.

SCOTTSDALE ARIZONA USA

A Note to the Reader

This publication is designed to provide accurate and authoritative information about the subject matters covered. It is sold with the understanding that neither the author nor publisher are rendering legal, mental health, medical or other professional services, either directly or indirectly. If expert assistance, legal services or counseling is needed, the services of a competent professional should be sought. Names and identifying information of private individuals have been changed to preserve anonymity. Neither the authors nor the publisher shall be liable or responsible for any loss or damage allegedly arising as a consequence of your use or application of any information or suggestions in this book.

ISBN-13: 978-1-936268-04-7

Library of Congress Control Number: 2013939699

Second edition.

Ordering and Contact Information

High Conflict Institute/New Ways for Families
Phone: 619-221-9108
Email: info@NewWays4Families.com
Website: NewWays4Families.com

This book is printed on acid-free paper.

Published by High Conflict Institute Press
www.hcipress.com
Printed in the United States of America

CONTENTS

INTRODUCTION

New Ways for Families™ is an exciting new method for handling the growing problem of high-conflict families in our courts and out of court, including in Collaborative Divorce and Parenting Coordination cases. It is designed to save courts time, to save parents money, and to protect children as their families re-organize in new ways after a separation or divorce, for married or never-married parents.

This interdisciplinary approach requires the cooperation and coordination of all professionals in addressing clients inside or outside the court process. The counseling/coaching component is brief and highly structured. It gives parents a chance to focus on learning skills to make positive changes rather than becoming preoccupied with defending themselves in the endless "attack-defend" cycle of parenting evaluation and litigation. It can be a partial assessment tool for future parenting orders. It gives parents a chance to change.

New Ways for Families requires a significant shift in attitude toward potentially high-conflict clients. Judges need to emphasize validating and motivating clients for future change, rather than criticizing past behavior -- while still making findings and orders about past behavior when necessary. Lawyers need to focus their clients on identifying and presenting neutral information about parenting behavior problems. Therapists need to be less involved in court decision-making, and more involved in counseling clients to overcome barriers to learning new skills. Parents need to be more involved in presenting neutral behavioral information and demonstrating their own new skills in court and out of court.

There are growing indications that many judges, lawyers, therapists and parents are ready for such a change in the family court process.

In further development of this method, High Conflict Institute now offers the New Ways method in many models, allowing for implementation in any setting, with any type of parent. There are now several approaches to using New Ways:

(1) Court Ordered,

(2) Attorney-Initiated,

(3) Mediation,

(4) Pre-Mediation Coaching,

(5) Parent-Initiated,

(6) Individual and Family Counseling,

(7) Collaborative Divorce, and

(8) Decision Skills Class.

NEW WAYS MODELS

There are several ways that the New Ways method can be used with potentially high-conflict families – or any family that wants to protect their children from conflict during or after their divorce. Parents or professionals can ask to use the New Ways method in any of the following models. Each model is structured around its own Workbook.

Court-Based Counseling

New Ways was specifically developed to help potentially high-conflict families that were active in the family court system. Ideally, judges, lawyers and counsellors receive training in the use of the method and the ways that each profession can reinforce the key skills that parents are taught in New Ways.

The method includes several paradigm shifts that only work if all professionals involved understand and reinforce the parents' skills at each step of the legal process.

By Court Order: Parents complete the full 12-week program with New Ways-trained therapists, or a counseling agency trained to use the New Ways method. This occurs before major decisions are made, ideally by agreement of the parents after completing the program, with or without the help of professionals. If unable to reach complete agreements, they return to court.

Voluntarily: Most high-conflict parents will not volunteer to help themselves. However, some parents may be able to complete the full 12 week program voluntarily, structured by a signed agreement, based upon the encouragement or recommendation of their lawyer, mediator, therapist or other family law professional..

Lawyers can encourage their clients to complete the counseling sessions while waiting for a court hearing or mediation. Court or private mediators can encourage their clients to participate in counseling either concurrently with mediation sessions, or after the first session and before returning for future sessions. Parenting Coordinators can also encourage or require their clients to complete the program upon assignment of the case. Therapists can work one-on-one with a client who wants to learn and practice the skills as part of private, individual therapy.

If there is a lower level of conflict, lawyers, mediators and parenting coordinators can also use the Pre-Mediation Coaching model with their clients, or refer them to the Decisions Skills class.

Collaborative Divorce

Collaborative Divorce professionals can encourage or require their clients to participate in the Collaborative model of New Ways. This model consists of three Individual Parent Coaching sessions (with the parents' Collaborative coaches) and three Parent-Child Coaching sessions (with the Child Specialist). The sessions are structured using the Collaborative Divorce Workbook. After completing New Ways, parents are better prepared to make decisions within the Collaborative Divorce framework. This may help parents stay in the collaborative process, who would otherwise drop out and go to court.

Decision Skills Class

The New Ways skills can be can be taught as three classes (60-90 minutes each), using the Decision Skills Workbook. This is a shorter version of the full 12 week program, but the focus remains on learning and practicing the four skills. It can also be incorporated into any existing parenting class curriculum.

Pre-Mediation Coaching

Mediators, lawyers or counselors can complete 1-2 coaching sessions with their clients prior to mediation, using the Pre-Mediation Coaching Workbook. This model is particularly beneficial for potentially high-conflict parents who would benefit from learning the skills prior to mediation, but do not require intensive counseling. Learning the skills prior to mediation should make for a more effective mediation process.

See subsequent chapters for detailed information on each model.

CHAPTER 1
Basic Structure and Skills

New Ways for Families is a short-term, 4-Step structured method for parents re-organizing their families after a separation or divorce. It is specifically designed to immunize parents and children against becoming high-conflict families in the family court system. It focuses on strengthening skills before making long-term decisions.

The first seven chapters of this Guidebook focus on the Court-Based model of *New Ways for Families*. Chapter Eight explains the Decision Skills Class model. Chapter Nine explains the Collaborative Divorce model. Chapter Ten explains the Parenting Coordination model. The remaining chapters are relevant to all models. All models include the same basic 4-Step structure, so that professionals are encouraged to read the entire Guidebook to understand the principles of New Ways and its significant differences from traditional methods of handling high-conflict families in divorce.

This method is designed to help parents immediately improve their skills, including families with allegations of child abuse, domestic violence, child alienation, substance abuse and false allegations. Chapters Thirteen and Fourteen explain of how New Ways can be used in these situations. The entire process is structured so that the parents never need to have direct contact, although that is an option by agreement of both parents. Temporary orders can be put in place, if needed, so that children and parents are protected and provided for while they are going through the New Ways method.

New Ways for Families can be used at any time by any family, from the beginning of the separation process or even after the divorce. While this method was developed for high-conflict family court cases, it can also be used in out-of-court settings, such as Collaborative Divorce, Divorce Mediation, and in negotiated divorce settlements with or without lawyers. After basic parenting decisions have been made, this method can also be used in conjunction with a Parenting Coordinator or individual or family counseling.

This Professional Guidebook describes the New Ways for Families method primarily in the context of a court case. However, alternatives for parents using this method out of court are explained as well. This chapter provides an overview and indicates the chapters which will further explain each step of the method and related issues.

Structure

Four Steps, with each step preparing parents for the next step. Ideally, this method should be 3-4 months from start to finish, including long-term parenting decisions by court order or agreement. The following is a brief overview of the 4 Steps, which are described in depth in the following chapters.

Step 1: Getting Started

Parents can agree to use New Ways, or a judge can order it while also making temporary orders (for parenting, support, protective orders, etc). Included in the order is the appointment of the Parent-Child Counselor for Step 3. Then, each parent selects his or her own Individual Parent Counselor for Step 2 from a list of counselors trained in the New Ways method, or is assigned a Parent Counselor by an participating counseling agency. Then, each parent prepares a Behavioral Declaration and a Reply Behavioral Declaration, which are the only declarations provided to the counselors, as well as any related parenting orders. See Chapter Four for more information about Step 1.

Step 2:   Individual Parent Counseling

This step includes 6 weekly sessions with a separate, confidential counselor for each parent using a Parent Workbook. Both parents participate in this counseling concurrently with their own counselor, with no presumptions about who is more difficult. The focus of these sessions is strengthening and practicing four conflict-reducing skills: flexible thinking, managed emotions, moderate behaviors and checking yourself. The counselor focuses on counseling and has no contact with the other counselor, an attorney for either parent, the Parent-Child Counselor or the court. This counselor signs a Verification of Completion when the client has finished the 6 sessions and completed the Individual Counseling section of the Parent Workbook. See Chapter Five for more information about Step 2. See Appendix V for sample Verification of Completion.

Step 3:   Parent-Child Counseling

This step includes 3 sessions with each parent and their child/ren, with the parents alternating weeks over six weeks. The parents share the same non-confidential counselor. They each complete the Parent-Child Counseling section of the Parent Workbook during these sessions. The Parent-Child Counselor does not write a report or make a recommendation, but can be called to testify at court regarding his or her observations, if a judge finds it necessary. The focus of these sessions is having the parents teach their children the same four skills they learned in their Individual Counseling, hearing the children's concerns, and discussing the new ways they will support each other in the new structure of their family. The Parent-Child Counselor may communicate with other professionals, including the parties' attorneys, mediators and the court. See Chapter Six for more information about Step 3. See Appendix V for sample Verification of Completion.

Step 4: Family (or Court) Decision-making

Finally, parents use their New Ways skills to develop a lasting parenting plan with the assistance of their attorneys (if any), a court mediator, a private mediator or a collaborative team. If they are unable to settle the case at this point, then they go to Family Court to report what they have learned. The judge will quiz each parent on how they would handle future parenting scenarios using their skills. Then the judge will hear the case, which may include testimony from the Parent-Child Counselor. The judge then orders long-term parenting, support, and other orders, which could include long-term restraining orders, batterers treatment, drug treatment, parenting class, a psychological evaluation, Guardian ad litem/minor's counsel, and/or a Parenting Coordinator, for assistance with handling future disputes. See Chapter Seven for more information.

Cost

The cost is paid by parents and varies by community standards for therapists. New Ways counselors should be specifically trained in the New Ways for Families method, and have experience with family court cases and the predictable problems of high-conflict parents. Therefore, each counselor or counseling agency determines their own fees, which may reflect their experience. Some jurisdictions are considering the use of low cost counselors associated with existing community services.

In San Diego County, a sliding fee scale is being used by some counselors in one out of every three of their New Ways cases. This scale ranges from $50 to $150 per hour for Individual Counselors and $100 to $200 per hour for Parent-Child Counselors. This results in a total cost of $600 - $1500 for each parent (6 individual sessions and 3 parent-child sessions per parent). This is not expensive, given the potential cost of high-conflict litigation to the parents and to the courts. ($600 is probably less than the cost of a single court hearing for most court systems.) If an agency provides trained counselors with a sliding scale, the cost could be even less.

Ideally, New Ways for Families reduces the number of court hearings and the use of court mediation services, by emphasizing out-of-court counseling at the front end of the court process before long-term decisions are made. If the parents are successful, they will be able to make their own decisions and can cancel scheduled court mediations and/or hearings. Given the structure of *New Ways for Families*, there should be no need to have numerous hearings simply to order one party into counseling or to cooperate with the counseling. Also, parents would be more likely to participate regularly in the counseling steps, because the end of the method includes a scheduled court hearing (unless they agree to cancel it). If a parent misses or delays counseling appointments, then the court will be informed of this at the planned hearing, rather than having to schedule a specific hearing to address this problem.

Goals

New Ways for Families has five basic goals, which may or may not apply to each specific family:

To immunize families against becoming high-conflict families during the separation or divorce, by teaching parents to avoid the three most common characteristics of high-conflict families: all-or-nothing thinking, unmanaged emotions, and extreme behaviors. Instead, they learn or strengthen skills of flexible thinking, managed emotions, and practicing moderate behaviors.

To help parents teach their children resilience in this time of huge and rapid change in the foundation of their family life. For children, they still have a family – a significantly reorganized family. Parents teach their children the same specific lessons about flexible thinking, managed emotions, and moderate behaviors, while also showing resilience by applying these lessons themselves.

To strengthen both parents' abilities to make parenting decisions, while relying less on experts and the courts to make their decisions for them.

To assist professionals and the courts in assessing each parent's potential to learn new, positive ways of problem-solving and organizing their family after a separation or divorce. By having both parents participate in New Ways, it helps professionals and the courts avoid creating an "all-bad parent" and an "all-good parent," which often escalates the family into high-conflict behavior.

To give parents a chance to change in court cases of abuse or alienation, before making long-term court orders which may limit their contact with children or require additional treatment (batterers treatment, drug treatment, further counseling, etc.). The New Ways method recognizes that one parent may have engaged in more negative behavior than the other. This method keeps the emphasis on both parents learning new skills for the future and teaching those skills to their child/ren, even while a parent may have limited contact.

NEW WAYS FOR FAMILIES - Sample "Court" Timeline

Any time a parent seeks restrictions on the other parent's contact with the children, or parents agree to use structured, short-term counseling for their family in transition:

Day 1 STEP 1A: court order (by stipulation or court order)

Court (or parents) appoint Parent-Child Counselor and set counseling deadlines; judge makes temporary orders as needed, possibly including temporary restraining orders, temporary parenting plans and temporary support, and date to return to court.

Week 1 STEP 1B: INDIVIDUAL PARENT COUNSELOR selected by each parent and **STEP 1C: BEHAVIORAL DECLARATION and REPLY** prepared by each parent, to be provided to Individual Counselor and to other parent (to provide to his/her counselor). Ideally, each parent retains an attorney or consults for assistance with this.

Week 2-7 STEP 2: INDIVIDUAL PARENT COUNSELING

Each parent meets with own confidential counselor for 6 sessions. If parents agree, the 6th session can be a joint session. Parent should complete counseling in Week 7, even if two sessions needed in some weeks to make up missed sessions by client or therapist, so both parents get Verifications of Completion and start Parent-Child Counseling in

Week 8 [RETURN TO COURT OPTION:

If highly restrictive parenting orders (no contact, very   limited hours, etc.), court can schedule parents to return to court at this point to re-evaluate temporary orders and possibly make new orders. MEDIATION OPTION: In some cases, meet with a mediator now to see if parents can make agreements.]

Week 8-13 STEP 3: PARENT-CHILD COUNSELING

Parents each have 3 sessions with the child/ren with the non-confidential counselor, alternating weeks so the children hear the same message reinforced by each parent before moving on to the next topic. When done, Counselor signs Verifications for each parent, schedules, communication methods, and future decision-making methods), with/

through their lawyers, a court mediator (FCS), a private mediator, or a collaborative divorce team.

Week 15 : [OPTIONAL ADDITIONAL PARENT-CHILD COUNSELING SESSION:

If parents mutually agree, parents meet separately or jointly for additional session with child/ren and Parent-Child Counselor to explain new ways they agree the family will operate: parenting schedules, communication methods, and future decision-making.]

Week 16 :

Or step 4 : court DECISION-MAKING HEARING

If parents can't reach an agreement: Judge quizzes parents on the skills they learned, quizzes them on hypothetical future parenting scenarios to see what they have absorbed, THEN gives tentative opinion and again encourages settlement.

If no agreement, THEN Judge hears testimony and argument; THEN makes long-term orders including parenting schedules, restraining orders, batterers treatment, drug treatment, parenting classes, more counseling, and/or appoints psychological evaluator, Guardian ad litem/Minor's Counsel, Parenting Coordinator, etc.

Research Basis

New Ways for Families draws upon recent research and principles drawn from Parent-Child Interaction Therapy (PCIT), Child-Inclusive Mediation, Dialectical Behavior Therapy (DBT), and Cognitive-Behavioral Therapy (CBT). Recent research indicates that many people with difficult and abusive personalities can change with 1) lots of structure; 2) small skills taught in small steps; 3) focus on future behavior, and 4) lots of validation from everyone working with them. Research also shows that working with parents and children together is more effective than working with them individually. See Chapter Eleven for more information about the research drawn upon in developing New Ways for Families.

Adaptation for Specific Cases and Budgets

The basic 4-Step structure of this method can be adapted by agreement of the parents or by the courts or the counseling agency providing the services, while retaining its basic structure and goals. Several adaptations are described in Chapter Twelve, including Collaborative Divorce, Mediation, and the Decision Skills Class.

No Major Court Changes Required

New Ways for Families does not require any major changes in family court procedures or laws. Most states and provinces already have laws regarding court-ordered counseling and/or parent education. When courts do not have the authority to order such a program, they can strongly encourage both parents to participate, as part of assisting the court before making appropriate long-term parenting orders.

Abuse and Alienation Issues

Most high-conflict family court cases include allegations of child abuse, domestic violence, child alienation, and/or false allegations. These allegations are extremely hard to analyze in the emotional heat of family court litigation and psychological evaluations. Experts may arrive at opposite conclusions about the same case, as they try to assess past behavior which no one observed except the parties. New Ways for Families can be a helpful partial assessment tool in observing each parent's ability to reflect on his or her own behavior, and ability to change negative behaviors.

Child abuse and child alienation are two of these common issues, which often are alleged at the same time ("he's abusing the children" vs. "she's alienating them"). Some parents in New Ways will be motivated to make changes, while others may be unable to make changes. Parents who are unable to change their future behavior should become more obvious to the court with this method, and appropriate orders can be made.

The issue of child alienation is particularly complicated and controversial. It often grows during a high-conflict court case, as blame escalates in litigation. Research shows that emotions are contagious, especially anxious emotions. New Ways is designed to reduce the risk of alienation by intervening early in a potentially high-conflict court case and lowering the parents' anxious emotions, even while one may have temporary restrictions on his or her parenting. New Ways engages both parents more fully in learning skills and in making decisions. It teaches methods for managing their own upset emotions and protecting their children from over-exposure to their upset emotions. For more information on how to handle the issues of abuse and alienation in New Ways, see Chapter Thirteen.

Domestic Violence

The Wingspread Conference about domestic violence, and its subsequent reports and articles, have had a positive impact on family law. Family law professionals are beginning to distinguish among different types of intimate partner violence, including: (1) an ongoing pattern of power and control, (2) incidents of violence which are mutually caused, or (3) a single incident or two at the time of separation without a pre-existing pattern. Working with both parents from the start should help reduce future risks, by helping perpetrators work on their own skills for managing their own behavior, and helping victims regain assertive skills and strengthen boundaries with the other party. New Ways is very compatible as a supplement to batterer's treatment and anger management programs.

As parents prepare their Behavioral Declarations with their lawyers or on their own, and move through Steps 2 and 3 of New Ways, they should begin separating out their own emotions from describing the other's behavior. With less of a preoccupation with the past, perpetrators of some family violence will be able to admit that their past behavior needs to be changed and make positive efforts to change it — rather than becoming mired in defending or denying their past behavior. Victims of family violence may be more able to become assertive and use the Individual Parent Counselor as a base for resisting patterns of returning to an abusive partner. For more information on how to handle domestic violence in New Ways, see Chapter Fourteen.

Training for Professionals

To be effective, New Ways for Families requires all professionals involved to have a shared basic knowledge of the method and a shared attitude of support for positive behavior change for those with personality disorders or traits. Professionals who work with family court cases should be well-informed about the dynamics and the many common pitfalls of high-conflict cases. They should have a level of comfort working with high-conflict people, so that they can avoid over-reacting to high-conflict behavior. This takes training and much practice.

High Conflict Institute provides basic and advanced training for therapists, lawyers and judges. For more information about New Ways training for professionals, see Chapter Seventeen.

Parent Workbooks

At the core of the New Ways for Families full 12 week program is the Parent Workbook, to be completed in Step 2 and Step 3. Each parent should receive separate copies of the Parent workbook. All professionals working with this method should be familiar with the workbooks, as they structure the sessions and the lessons to be learned and reinforced by all professionals involved. Professionals working with clients in Collaborative Divorce will use the Collaborative Parent Workbook. Professionals working with clients in the Decision Skills Class model will use the Decision Skills Workbook. Professionals working with clients using the Pre-Mediation Coaching model will use the Pre-Mediation Coaching Workbook. All workbooks contain similar practice exercises, but have been adapted specifically for each of these models.

Parent-Child Counseling Rather Than Individual Child Therapy

One of the big differences in New Ways for Families from other family court approaches to high-conflict families is the emphasis on parent-child therapy. Individual therapy for the child has generally not proven successful in resolving the problems of child abuse and/or child alienation—because these are not the child's responsibility, but rather family systems' problems and parent skills problems. Often an individual child therapist becomes persuaded by the child or one of the parents to take an advocacy role against the other parent. See Chapter Eleven about the success of Parent-Child Interaction Therapy as an example of an existing program which focuses on conjoint counseling for abusive families.

Children necessarily adapt to their parents' dysfunction and become an essential part of the dysfunctional family system. Therefore, the system of both of them needs to be treated together, rather than separately. Also, children and parents often pressure the individual child therapist to adopt an all-or-nothing view of the family in many cases, and the structure of individual child therapy reinforces this. Even when this pressure does not occur, the therapist still has much less influence on how the child thinks than his or her parents.

Therefore, by focusing instead on conjoint parent-child counseling, the therapist facilitates the parents in teaching the child new ways of handling family problems. For the child, hearing new ways of thinking about the other parent and dealing with the other parent—coming from each parent—is much more powerful than just hearing it from a therapist. For the parents, hearing their child/ren's own concerns directly has been shown to be much more persuasive than generic parenting education about generic children. See Chapter Eleven regarding Child-Inclusive Divorce Mediation. Individual child therapy may be appropriate after the New Ways for Families method has been completed.

Empowering Parents

Rather than ordering individual therapy in isolation for each parent in the family, New Ways for Families focuses the therapy on the parent-child relationship directly. The parents' therapy prepares them for the parent-child therapy. They learn how to teach the child/ren themselves, rather than having professionals do it for them. It also gives them motivation for learning skills quickly, as new parenting orders may be made as soon as 12 weeks later, if they can demonstrate sufficient progress.

Rather than vague orders for counseling (often with the length of the therapy to be determined by the therapist), the New Ways for Families approach is time-limited. After 6 weeks, a parent can choose to continue with his or her individual confidential therapist, without the therapist being tainted by court involvement. After 6 weeks with the parent-child counselor, the parents can return to this counselor in the future for assistance with the child/ren, if needed.

An Innovative Method

In short, New Ways for Families is designed to reduce the adversarial pressure on high-conflict parents enough for them to learn new skills. It includes the following shifts in emphasis from the existing family court approaches, which have failed worldwide:

Ordering counseling which focuses on learning new skills, rather than focusing vaguely on healing the divorce or addressing specific past bad behavior. They need new skills first, before they can heal the divorce or address past bad behavior productively.

Ordering both parents into New Ways for Families at the start, rather than focusing on one parent as bad, to avoid escalating the case into high conflict with a "winner" and a "loser" at the very first hearing. Temporary protective orders and temporary restricted parenting schedules could still be ordered, without prejudice.

Providing a structured, time-limited counseling process (12 weeks).

Engaging parents in counseling when they are most motivated, rather than after big decisions are made when they are most defensive, non-compliant, and preoccupied with reversing negative court decisions. Removing the Individual Counselors from the court battle by making the Individual Counseling confidential. This puts the burden on the parents to learn skills and report back to court, rather than hooking the counselor into writing a letter to the court or simply supporting the parent's viewpoint.

Focusing on Parent-Child Counseling, rather than individual child counseling, in this front-end process. This teaches parents to teach their children positive skills from the start of the litigation process. This reduces the risk of alienation growing from negative statements and negative emotions during a high-conflict case.

Emphasizing positive encouragement by the courts and attorneys for parents learning new ways, rather than emphasizing negative feedback (while still making necessary findings). Recent research on treating borderline and narcissistic personality disorders has proven that validating the person (not the behavior) is necessary before they can learn new behaviors.

Providing skills for parents to make their own decisions before locking parents into high-conflict litigation behavior by preparing for court mediation and/or highly-contested court hearings from the start. (Family Court Services or other mediation could occur after Steps 2 or 3 of counseling. This may reduce the use of court mediation as well.)

Making court parenting decisions based on each parent's ability to learn using the observations of the Parent-Child Counselor, rather than focusing as much time on past behavior which no one else observed and is highly-contested. The Parent-Child Counselor would not be confidential and could testify.

Assessing the level of domestic violence, child abuse and child alienation after giving the parents a chance to acknowledge and start changing past behavior. This recognizes the concerns which arose out of the Wingspread Conference on domestic violence and screening cases for different types and levels of violence. After 12 weeks, it would be clearer to the court which cases needed further investigation by appointing a Guardian ad litem or Minor's Counsel and/or a psychological evaluator. Cases which needed batterers' treatment, anger management or more counseling, should be more obvious.

Summary

The focus of New Ways for Families is on learning new ways (new skills) of thinking, managing emotions and behaving, while the parents and children adjust to the new ways that their family is organized after a separation or divorce. While the court will acknowledge and may make formal findings about past inappropriate behaviors, the emphasis is on learning new ways. This avoids the endless "attack and defend" cycle of high-conflict divorce cases regarding what each party did or said in the past.

The benefit of New Ways for Families is that it immediately shifts the focus onto the future and learning new behavior, rather than focusing on the past. If possible, it should be ordered as soon as a parent or the court is concerned that one or both parents need restrictions placed on their parenting (no contact, supervised access, or very limited time) because of past parenting behavior. Often the beginning of the case is when parents are most motivated to change and not yet deeply engaged in the negative cycle of preparing attack and defend declarations/affidavits.

Even after a separation or divorce case may be "over," parents may benefit from New Ways for Families at any time. Even when there is no case in family court, families can use New Ways for Families as a method to help them deal with economic changes, moving out of a familiar home, moving of out of a familiar community, returning after military service overseas, or any other significant changes causing a family to operate in new ways.

CHAPTER 2
How Judges Provide The Structure

Judges are the key to the success of the New Ways for Families method with high-conflict cases. Judges provide the necessary structure that high-conflict families need and can't provide for themselves. Ordinarily, legal professionals assume a level of self-awareness and self-management for parties in civil cases, so that once court decisions are made the individuals involved will implement the court's orders and go on living their lives in a responsible manner.

In this regard, New Ways for Families is a paradigm shift for judicial officers and all professionals involved in family cases. High-conflict families tend to be driven by one or two parties with high-conflict personalities. Dysfunction and high-conflict behavior are part of who they are. They are experienced at adversarial processes (like court), but without resolution. They cannot be talked out of their life-long personalities. They need a significantly different approach, based on principles of treatment for those with personality disorders or traits.

Requiring the Learning of Skills

New Ways for Families teaches potentially high-conflict parents small conflict resolution skills in small steps with lots of repetition and validation. Then every professional that deals with them needs to reinforce the use of these skills whenever decisions need to be made. When the court process is properly structured in this manner, even high-conflict parents are able to make their decisions out of court. These skills aren't parenting skills per se (although they improve parenting), but rather four key conflict resolution or conflict management skills:

flexible thinking (such as making proposals and responding to proposals),

managed emotions (such as telling yourself encouraging statements),

moderate behaviors (such as brief, informative, friendly and firm emails), and

checking yourself (for using these skills rather than focusing on other people).

By learning these skills, parents become more able to participate in making their own decisions, more likely to accept their own decisions and more positive in managing their children during and after the divorce. In the small percentage of cases where they are still unable to make their own decisions and the judge has to make the decisions for them, these skills generally help them reduce the level of family conflict and make them more likely to accept court decisions.

Providing Structure

Rather than lecturing or coaxing or making long explanations to high-conflict parents, judges are far more effective by ordering a **court-ordered structure** at the start of a potentially high-conflict case for learning the above skills over a short period of time. This involves three components:

Careful Explanation of the court order and the steps of the structure (individual counseling followed by parent-child counseling, followed by decision-making) and the tasks they must do to get started (Step 1): Selecting their own counselor, writing a 2-page Behavioral Declaration for the counselors, and scheduling appointments to start right away.

Setting Deadlines for accomplishing each step of the structure and writing them in the court order. This is necessary because high-conflict people are generally focused on the present and are not thinking ahead. When the judge makes this important, then the parties take it more seriously than when a lawyer or counselor simply tells them.

Setting a Hearing to follow the deadlines for completion. This is an absolute necessity, otherwise high-conflict parents have no incentive to learn skills and change behavior. Remember, they are not self-structuring – understanding this is the main paradigm shift of New Ways for Families – so that they need this external structure to accomplish difficult tasks (see explanation below about the Bar Exam).

Motivational Comments should immediately follow the making of this order, with judges explaining both positive and negative consequences to the parents for following the structure. Positive consequences include improving their own relationships with their children and managing their relationship with each other better as co-parents (even if the other parent is difficult and they have no direct contact). Positive consequences also include being able to make their own decisions after the New Ways process, or, if they return to court, being able to show their skills to the judge. Negative consequences include negative decisions by the court at the scheduled hearing, if it becomes clear that they have learned nothing and have not made any efforts to improve their skills. If they are able to make their own parenting plan decisions, then they will not need this hearing. But they must know that it is hanging there over their heads if they don't make their own decisions.

A Skills-Focused Structure

Without such a skills-focused structure, judges just make decisions for high-conflict parents, which they generally ignore, undermine or challenge again and again in court. When the court just makes decisions for these parents, no skills are learned and their children continue to experience the chaos of their parents' endless battles in and out of court. New Ways for Families is designed to block this high-conflict behavior by teaching and expecting the use of these four skills – something positive to do, instead of just not behaving badly. If you don't replace negative behavior with something positive, the negative will resume in short order.

Therefore, the first step of New Ways for Families is Getting Started, including this clear court order made with motivational comments and a hearing scheduled at the end. This step of "Getting Started" is the most important step, in that the judge ties the learning of skills to the decision-making process.

While it may seem cumbersome at the beginning, high-conflict parents need such a structure because for psychological reasons they sabotage their own goals and strongly resist changing their own behavior – even when it would help them. They lack the relationship conflict skills necessary to manage themselves when they are defensive, which is much of the time. They need a fairly simple, but strong, method to overcome this internal resistance and engage in learning.

Part of this structure is having several counseling sessions. This is because a standard parenting class does not teach relationship skills the way that individual counseling can, because it is a relationship within which to practice communicating and making decisions. Several sessions are needed to reinforce the skills and to ground them in the parent's memory of a positive relationship experience, which many of them have not had for a long time, if ever.

Part of the structure is having a Parent Workbook. This workbook provides tasks for the counseling sessions, so the parents know what they are supposed to learn and it can be discussed and reinforced over and over again with their counselor. Then, all professionals in the case know what they were supposed to learn and can reinforce the skills whenever they come into contact and a decision needs to be made.

Like a Bar Exam

An essential part of the structure for parents is knowing that the court is personally invested in their success, and that there will be a court hearing at the end, unless they reach their own agreements before the court date. The best analogy for judges and lawyers for this scheduled court hearing from the start is the bar exam. Lawyers and judges would not have studied day and night for weeks and weeks, if they didn't know they were going to have the bar exam at the end of the process. Just consider that it is harder for a high-conflict parent to change their own behavior than it is for a law student to pass the bar exam. High-conflict people have to have the expectation that they are going to be questioned on the skills that they are learning at the end of the process, or they won't even try.

Most people are familiar with how hard it is for an alcoholic or addict to learn the skills to stay clean and sober without a strong structure, such as a treatment program or 12-step program. Changing one's personality-based behavior is even harder. Giving potentially high-conflict parents a strong structure with a quiz at the end of the process helps them to help themselves. Will power and logic just don't do it, or they wouldn't be in court in their 20's, 30's, 40's and even older.

Mediation or Other Negotiation Process

Step 4 of New Ways for Families is the decision-making process. Mediation is ideal for this purpose, with a mediator trained to guide the parents in using their New Ways skills to manage their emotions, to communicate sufficiently, to make proposals and to make decisions. Other negotiation methods can be just as effective, such as a collaborative divorce team or cooperative attorneys, so long as they have been trained to reinforce the New Ways skills, rather than just pushing the parties to accept the professionals' points of view.

It is important not to give up right away in using these out-of-court methods, as it often takes high-conflict people two or three times as long to actually make agreements that will stick. They often struggle with finalizing their agreements. Yet it is far better for them to struggle along using their skills, so that they get the credit for the final result – and it lasts. Otherwise, they won't follow these agreements. It's a delicate balance, which is why training is so important.

The New Ways Quiz

In the event that parents are unable to learn and practice sufficient skills to reach their own decisions in mediation or other dispute resolution process, then they face their court hearing. However, this must also be part of the overall structure, otherwise the parents will not apply what they have learned to future problem-solving. Therefore, there are several steps the court must emphasize in running this hearing, so that parents will work harder in the process.

Quiz the Parents on what they have learned. The judge expects each parent to explain how he or she is practicing at least one of the following: managed emotions, flexible thinking, moderate behaviors or checking themselves. Then, they are praised for their efforts and the court points out how these will help them in the future, in their own lives as well as teaching their children how to manage conflict.

Provide a Hypothetical Parenting Scenario and ask each of them how they would deal with this situation in the future using their skills. It should be similar to a problem situation they had in the past. This will help the court see how much they have really learned, and whether they can apply what they say they have learned.

Provide a Tentative Opinion based on what the judge has learned about each parent is able to use their skills. (This may include a short written statement of observations from the New Ways Parent-Child Counselor, but not as an expert opinion or recommendations – just observations as a counselor.)

Encourage them to Negotiate Again out in the hallway after they hear the court's tentative opinion. There should be motivational comments again about the positive consequences of negotiating their own agreements versus the negative consequences of having the judge make them instead. If they return with some agreements, praise their efforts and send them back out try again to finish with a complete agreement. Remember that high-conflict people generally take longer to reach agreements.

If All Else Fails, then the parties will have a normal hearing or trial.

Conclusion

This structure may appear rigid and detailed at the beginning and end of the case (and sometimes at a brief motivational hearing in the middle). However, when followed it has already been demonstrating its potential for success in several jurisdictions. New Ways for Families helps high-conflict families stay out of court, even when they started out in court and were headed toward becoming long-term cases with many future hearings. This method is saving court hearings and overall court costs. Plus, the parents learn conflict resolution skills (or "conflict management" skills) that they can use anywhere and teach to their own children for their own future relationships and families.

CHAPTER 3
Model Court Case Example

The following hypothetical example is based on real facts from ordinary cases and demonstrates how the 4 Steps of the New Ways for Families method can work in Family Courts. This example includes the issues high-conflict parents often raise (domestic violence, child abuse, and child alienation), and the focus on skills and validating responses that all professionals can provide. The subsequent chapters explain the steps of the method and the roles of each professional. This chapter shows how the court controls the process, using a tone that motivates change while setting limits. [Steps of the New Ways method are in brackets, for reference to Ch. 1 Timeline.]

"My Husband hit my son with a belt a week ago, because he wouldn't do his homework," Sara Turell told her divorce lawyer, Mr. Benjamin, over the phone. "So this past weekend I wouldn't let him have the children when he came to the house. He started screaming and pounded on my front screen door so hard that it fell off one of its hinges! I was in fear for my life and I called the police. They told him to leave and gave me a 5-day temporary protective order, but they said I need to get a protective order in the Family Court. You have to help protect me and the children from their father. I don't know what he'll do next!"

Sara and Brad Turell were married for 12 years, before they separated January 3rd, right after New Years. He told her he wanted a divorce and she was devastated. She told him to stay away from her, their house, and their two children, Tommy, age 13, and Tara, age 8, until she figured out what to do. Brad went to stay with a friend from work. The prior weekend was his first contact with the children since he left the house.

"That's terrible," said Mr. Benjamin. "I'll have him served with the divorce papers and give him notice of an emergency hearing, where we'll request a protective order against him coming near you and against him seeing the kids until this gets sorted out. Come in at 3pm today, so I can prepare your affidavit/declaration. We'll file your Petition and ask for a Protective Order on Wednesday."

The First Court Hearing –[Step 1A: Court Order]

Judge Alan B. Clements: "This is the case of Brad and Sara Turell. I see that Ms. Turell has filed for a hearing on custody, visitation, and child support and that you are requesting emergency protective orders against Mr. Turell and a No Contact order between Mr. Turell and the minor children. I have read your documents and heard brief testimony from each of you. Here are my temporary orders:

"I am going to approve your request for a temporary protective order, Ms. Turell, based on the belt incident and the door incident. Mr. Turell is ordered to stay 100 yards away from the residence, from you and from the children, until the next hearing. However, I find no basis to deny contact with the children and will authorize supervised visitation with the children with a professional supervisor two days a week, for two hours each visit.

"I also want both of you to participate in *New Ways for Families*, before the next court hearing. This is a new program of counseling to be completed before final decisions are made. You each have your own confidential counselor for six individual sessions over six weeks. Then you will each have three sessions with your children, with a shared Parent-Child Counselor. Then I'd like to have an interim hearing in eight weeks so you will have adequate time to complete your first six sessions. This is a longer wait than usual before a full hearing on a protective order, but I believe that the work you do in this short-term counseling will help you both immediately – and help you learn skills to help your children be resilient through your separation and divorce. It will also help me in making my decisions at the next hearing.

"So I will need your agreement, Mr. Turell, to extend the next hearing date for eight weeks, because you have a right to a speedy hearing. I understand that you won't see your children much during this time, but if the counseling is productive, you should have much more contact after that and it may not need to be supervised. If I have to make a decision sooner, I may be less comfortable making any changes. Do you agree, Mr. Turell, to extending the court hearing eight weeks, to allow time to attend this counseling in the meantime?"

Brad: "Yes, but she's exaggerating what happened! The screen door was already loose and she wasn't afraid at all! She's just lying to cut me off from my kids. When the police came, I cooperated and left. But as I was leaving, she yelled 'Get out of our lives! The kids don't want to see you anymore!' The kids were there and saw and heard everything."

Judge Clements: "Thank you, Mr. Turell. I'll hear the details of what happened at the next hearing. In the meantime, I'm ordering you both to attend *New Ways for Families*. You will each select your own Individual Parent Counselor, who is completely confidential. Then, after our next hearing, you will each attend Parent-Child Counseling with the counselor I have selected, Mr. Desjardins who will meet with each of you separately with your children. I'm appointing Mr. Desjardins, who won't be confidential. He won't serve as an expert and won't make recommendations. But I can ask him questions about what was observed with each of you during the counseling with your children, if necessary, so long as you both sign releases. But hopefully, by then, you will both be able to develop your own parenting plan, so I might not even need to see you again."

"Your Honor, may I speak?" Mr. Benjamin inquired.

"Yes, go ahead Mr. Benjamin," Judge Clements replied, looking up from his notes.

Mr. Benjamin proceeded: "Ms. Turell prefers that she not be required to attend *New Ways for Families*, as she has not been abusive with the children herself."

Judge Clements responded: "I can understand that you might feel that way, Ms. Turell. New Ways is not a punishment or treatment program for abuse. It's a 6 week series of counseling sessions, each parent with their own confidential counselor, to discuss new ways to adjust to changes in your family. New Ways for Families is routinely ordered for both parents, so that you are both learning the same methods to then teach your children in order to help them adjust to all of these changes. At the next hearing, it will help me to see what each of you have learned. It will also help you both support each other as parents, as your children do indeed need both of you. Even people who aren't in court use New Ways for Families for separation and divorce."

"So I'm ordering you both to select your Individual Parent Counselor from this list that we maintain within the next 7 days. Then, you should each prepare a Behavioral Declaration to provide to your Counselor and to the other parent, who will provide it to his or her Counselor. You can get blank declaration forms and instructions from the New Ways for Families website. I'm also scheduling a hearing in 8 weeks. Good luck to you both."

[See Appendix I for a blank court order and above court order, including deadlines]

Selecting an Individual Parent Counselor [Step 1B]

"Here's the current list of counselors trained in the New Ways for Families method," Mr. Benjamin explained to Sara back at his office. "You'll each choose your own Individual Parent Counselor, schedule your own appointments, and you'll each make your own payment arrangements with your counselor. You need to make contact this week, so you can start next week or as soon as possible. As long as it's from this list, it's entirely up to you who you choose. Although, I can recommend a few counselors I've had a good experience with in similar cases."

Preparing a Behavioral Declaration and Reply [Step 1C]

"And here's the instructions for preparing a Behavioral Declaration," he told Sara. ""With a Behavioral Declaration, we tell the counselors in neutral and descriptive terms what Brad's behavior problems are as a parent. The idea is to think about behavior, rather than who's a good parent and who's a bad parent. That way, the counselors can help each of you learn new ways of dealing with each other and the children.

"So while you might want to say that Brad is a raging maniac, what you put in the Behavioral Declaration is a one-paragraph description of his actual behavior, how frequent this type of behavior is, and what orders you are requesting to address this behavior.

"Also, we need to say if this is an on-going pattern of behavior for him. Complete this declaration to the best of your ability. Brad gets to do one as well about your behaviors as a parent, and then you each do a Reply Behavioral Declaration to say whether you agreed with the problems the other parent identified, or not. It doesn't have to be perfect. It just helps the counselors help both of you."

"So, tell me now in neutral and descriptive terms what your three biggest concerns are about Brad's parenting behavior."

Sara replied: "Well, he's really abusive and unreasonable with the children. He makes them do things they don't want to do."

"So, can you describe his exact behavior?"

"Yes, he tells our son that he has to do a woodworking project with him, but Tommy really hates doing those projects with him because of his dad's temper." Sara said.

"So," Mr. Benjamin replied, "You could say: 'Mr. Turell says to Tommy that he has to spend time on a woodworking project with his father. When Tommy says 'No,' his father still requires him to do this.'" "What does his father do if he refuses to work on a woodworking project? And what kind of project is it?" he asked.

"Well, Tommy never says 'No.' I think it's because he's afraid to. I can just see it in his face, but his father doesn't. He made Tommy help him build a bird house a few months ago. Tommy just went along with him," Sara said. "But he feels under a lot of pressure."

"What about hitting Tommy with a belt? Has that happened before?"

"Once before, a couple years ago," Sara replied. "It was about homework that time too, when I was out of town for a couple days. It's only a problem now, because I'm not around when he has visitation with the children where he's staying. When I'm around, I usually help with their homework. After all, Brad's just a janitor and I have a Master's degree."

"Okay," Mr. Benjamin replied. "Tell me in descriptive terms what happened a couple years ago: WHO did WHAT, WHERE, WHEN, and HOW it affected the children."

[See Appendix II for Sara's Behavioral Declaration, as well as Brad's, and both of their Reply Behavioral Declarations.]

New Ways Individual Parent Counseling [Step 2]

With the counselor Brad selected, Dr. Simon, he wanted to complain a lot about Sara, but Dr. Simon kept the focus on setting his own goals, discussing his strengths, and writing about "all-or-nothing thinking" and "flexible thinking" in his Parent Workbook. As Brad got used to his counselor, he asked him to write a letter to the court on his behalf. However, Dr. Simon reminded him that the Individual counseling is completely confidential and that he was forbidden from writing to the court or discussing the case with any other professional. The burden was on Brad to learn how to handle things and to explain to the court what he had learned.

Over the next few weeks, Brad talked about how emotions sometimes overwhelm him. He explained how his father used to punish him with a belt if he didn't study. He graduated high school, but never wanted to go further. He was satisfied with his job as a janitor at the local high school. But Brad wanted Tommy and Tara to study and go to college, and he felt competitive with his wife, who had a Master's degree.

On the other hand, he really enjoyed woodworking, and he liked doing woodworking projects with his son and daughter. The kids really seemed to love doing these projects with him. Throughout these discussions with Dr. Simon, he worked on his workbook, gave examples of flexible thinking, discussed how to manage his emotions and ways he could support Sara's relationship with the children. He practiced what he would say to the judge about his past behavior of using his belt to get Tommy to study. He came to understand how that had hurt his relationship with his children and his position in court.

"Now that we're done with the six weeks of counseling, will you sign my Verification letter saying that I've completed this?" Brad asked Dr. Simon.

"Sure. This verifies that you completed six sessions and your Parent Workbook. You can show this to anyone you wish. Just remember that I will have no other communication with any other professional about my sessions with you. That keeps it really confidential. And if you ever want to come back again for another session or two, feel free to contact me. I think that you learned a lot that will help you in the future."

"Thanks. I think I'll remember the basics: flexible thinking, managed emotions, and moderate behaviors. Right?"

"You got it!" Dr. Simon said.

...

[Sara's counseling]

In her counseling, Sara blamed Brad 100% for the divorce. She said it caught her by surprise and she felt totally abandoned by him. The counselor she selected, Dr. Delisle, helped her focus back on what she could learn to help herself and the children through this difficult period. Handling her emotions was a real concern, as she was furious with Brad for disrupting her life. But she said she was not going to allow Brad to care for the children while she was working, when her stepmother was available and so much more competent.

In the counseling Sara learned tips for calming her own emotions so she would feel less overwhelmed. She also came to accept that Dr. Delisle could not testify at court on her behalf. She finally practiced what she would say at court about handling her own emotions, as she was starting to realize that the children were frightened by her intense sadness and anger about Brad.

She mentioned in one counseling session that her daughter, Tara, had said that she was scared by both of her parents' anger sometimes, but that she wanted to just live with her mother so the anger would stop. Tommy once told her he didn't want to see his father anymore because the divorce was all his father's fault.

Sara had a particularly hard time with the idea that she should support Brad as a parent. Despite her efforts to encourage a co-parenting relationship and flexible thinking, Sara said she would ask the court to stop the visitation – to not force the children to spend time with Brad anymore. She said it would just be so much easier without him being involved and that her stepmother could take care of the children when Sara wasn't available.

Dr. Delisle said that the court would probably get upset with her for taking this position, because the judge might consider this to be an example of "all-or-nothing thinking," rather than "flexible thinking." She asked if there were other, more flexible, ideas she might present to the court. Sara said she just couldn't cope with seeing Brad anymore and felt strongly that he was unable to be sensitive to the children's needs. Dr. Delisle didn't argue with her, but suggested that she might practice writing down a few other flexible proposals if the judge didn't like this one.

"Flexible thinking often takes a long time to learn," Dr. Delisle said. "Especially when it's about something as important as your children. These are hard and big decisions, and I know it's not easy. After the hearing, if you find that you would like another counseling session, feel free to contact me. I think that we have worked well together."

"Thanks, I'll consider that," said Sara. "You've made it easier for me and you haven't criticized me, like I thought you would."

Interim Court Hearing –Optional [After Step 2]

Judge Clements: "Welcome back, Mr. Turell, Ms. Turell, and Mr. Benjamin. What is the status of this case?"

Mr. Benjamin: "Both parents have attended New Ways for Families for 6 sessions each. However, there are no agreements at this time. And there's a new development since the last hearing. The children no longer want to visit at all with Mr. Turell. So my client is requesting that the visitation be stopped, until Mr. Turell gets some treatment for his abusive behavior with the children."

Judge Clements: "Okay, thank you Mr. Benjamin. Mr. Turell, I'm going to start with you. Tell me what you have learned in your counseling. Then I'm going to ask you for your response to what Mr. Benjamin has just said. But let's start with what you have learned."

Brad: "I've learned that I can't use a belt in disciplining my son about his homework, the way that my father used with me. Now it's considered child abuse. But I also realized that I let myself get too rigid about homework, and that I can actually help my children even though I don't have a Master's degree like their mother. If I start to get stressed, I can calm myself down by reminding myself that I'm a pretty good parent in many ways. During my supervised visits, I've really focused more on my children and what their interests are at this age. I was too uptight about competing with their mother and missed all the ways they enjoy being with me."

Judge Clements: "I'm very pleased that you have learned these things about yourself and your children. This will help over the years ahead. I'm glad you realize that using a belt is not moderate behavior. What would you do in the future if Ms. Turell refused to allow you to see the children? Would yelling and pounding on the door be moderate behavior in your eyes now? What could you do instead?"

Brad: "No, I know now that yelling and pounding on the door are not moderate behaviors. I'm checking myself now and before doing anything, I would call a lawyer I've been working with and ask her what to do. I wouldn't even go over to our house. I would calm myself and call the lawyer."

Judge Clements: "Good. I'm glad to hear you are checking yourself now. Now, how do you respond to Ms. Turell's statement that the children don't want to see you anymore?"

Brad: "That's totally false! It's been hard visiting with the children at the supervisor's place, but the children have enjoyed seeing me. They want to see me more, without someone watching over our shoulders. I really want to show you that normal time with my children will work out just fine.

"No one ever accused me of being abusive before. Even two years ago, Sara didn't call it abuse after the belt incident. She didn't call CPS and she didn't ask for restraining orders. She just said never to do that again. There's no reason I shouldn't have half of the parenting time. I used to care for the kids most of the time while Sara was getting her Master's degree, and she didn't complain then! The problem is that she tells them that they don't need me – she says that she and her stepmother are all they need."

Judge Clements: "Well, the report from the Visitation Supervisor says that the children responded well to you. Frankly, I'm surprised to hear that they told their mother that they don't want to see you.

"Now, Ms. Turell, tell me what you have learned in your New Ways Individual Parent Counseling, then tell me why you think the children don't want to spend time with their father."

Sara: "I've learned that I shouldn't express my sadness and anger about Mr. Turell around the children because it upsets them. I've learned that my feelings can be contagious, and that they may start feeling sad when I'm sad or angry. I've tried to just go into my room and cry or scream into a pillow with the door closed."

Judge Clements: "Thank you. I'm glad you learned about protecting the children from your upset feelings. It is very important for their future, to know that their parents can cope with big changes without sharing the full intensity of their upset emotions with them."

Sara: "The children don't want to see their father because he hit Tommy with a belt and he scared them when he pounded so hard on the screen door. They're scared of him even when they visit with him with that supervisor lady. They tell me that they're afraid of him now."

Judge Clements: "Thank you, Ms. Turell, for telling me what you've learned and why you think the children don't want to see their father. I've heard enough to make my new orders:

"I'm going to order you both to participate in New Ways Parent-Child Counseling for the next 6 weeks. The counselor will help you each teach your children how to stay resilient during the divorce, and hearing from them will help you develop a more solid parenting plan. Remember, a plan that you two develop is usually better than one that the court has to order. Also, I want to emphasize that the Parent-Child Counseling is not going to be confidential, unlike your individual counseling. The Parent-Child Counselor won't write a report, but if you don't reach an agreement I may want to hear this Counselor's observations during the counseling before I make my long-term decisions.

"I am also going to make a finding that there is a basis for a Restraining Order to remain in place, based on the belt incident and the door incident, but I am only going to order that for the next 6 months, to keep the peace while things settle down. Neither of you have reported a long-standing pattern of dangerous behavior."

"I am also concerned about the comments that Ms. Turell is making to the children. Your progress in New Ways for Families will also help me make appropriate orders."

"I am going to order normal, unsupervised visitation for Mr. Turell until the next hearing. Regardless of what the children say, neither parent has described a pattern of parenting behavior to justify no contact with their father, or even supervised visitation at this time. He'll have alternate weekends, Friday after school to Monday morning back to school; and every Wednesday from after school to Thursday mornings back to school. That way you won't interact with each other. Remember, there's still a restraining order in effect, although it is now revised to accommodate the new temporary parenting plan.

"After your Parent-Child Counseling, you will need to attempt to reach an agreement about your future parenting schedule and relationship. You will need to meet and confer with or through your attorney(s), and you are advised to obtain one Mr. Turell. If you can't reach an agreement, you will need to meet with a private mediator before our next hearing. I am going to schedule the next hearing for 10 weeks from now. That allows you enough time to attend your Parent- Child Counseling and to attempt to settle your case.

"If you haven't reached an agreement about a parenting plan that you can both agree to by then, I will make one for you. I may consider many possible parenting arrangements, as everything I have ordered so far has been temporary, and without prejudice to either party. I might order equal parenting time, or give one of you primary physical custody. I also may have to order a psychological evaluation, a parenting class, and/or more counseling. Remember, it is always best if the two of you can agree. Good Luck to you both."

New Ways Parent-Child Counseling [Step 3]

Sara met with the children first, with the Parent-Child Counselor, Mr. Desjardins. She struggled to explain to the children the important lessons she had learned in her counseling.

Sara: "We have to try to avoid "all-or-nothing thinking," she explained to the two children. "We have to use our flexible thinking. That means that we should think about many ways of dealing with problems. There's always more than one solution.

"We also have to remember that our feelings are just our feelings. Sometimes we don't even know the reasons we feel the way we do. If our feelings are too intense, then we should just walk away or tell ourselves something encouraging, like the Olympic athletes do."

Sara struggled with the part about supporting the other parent. She knew she was supposed to, but she really didn't want to. The Parent-Child Counselor pointed out that this was perhaps the most important part of the lessons to teach her children. Sara finally explained the following: "It's very hard for me to support your relationship with your father, when I see how upset you both are. I won't force you to see him, but the judge and the counselor might force you."

The Parent-Child Counselor intervened: "Try not to use the word 'force' in discussing this problem. It gives a negative feeling to spending time with their father and feelings are contagious. There are many things parents expect their children to do or not to do, because this is in their best interest. Like school, for example. Do you kids always want to go to school every day?" Mr. Desjardins asked the children.

"No way," Tommy exclaimed. "But my mom says we have to go, so we go. We know they want the best for us. I guess it's kind of like that about seeing our Dad, even if we don't always want to go."

"That's right," said Mr. Desjardins. "It's in your best interest. It's what all parents expect. Can you, Mom, tell them who decides whether they see their father or go to school? Is this something the children get to decide?"

"No," Sara replied. "This is something that's up to me and the judge. I'll try to convince the judge that you shouldn't have to go."

"Let's focus back on the workbook now," the counselor interrupted. "It's important for your children to know that they learn different things from each of you, and that both of you are important in their lives. Can you explain the reasons for that to the children?"

"Well," Sara replied. "I guess that they learn different things from each of us, but it's hard for me to see how you can learn anything from your father right now."

"Well," the counselor interjected. "Let's see if the children can help you. What do you think you have learned from your father?"

Tommy: "He's really taught me how to make things and how to be a boy around other boys. And how to stick up for myself."

"How about you, Tara?" the counselor continued.

"He taught me how to make a wooden box for my dolls," Tara replied. "And he takes me to my friends' houses for overnights. He likes to see me happy! He says we're the best part of his life."

"Sara, make sure to write down these comments in your workbook. It sounds like Brad may be more important to the children than you realized. Even though it's a hard time for you, it's important for them to stay connected. It will affect how they deal with other people during hard times in the future when they grow up. You might want to think about this before our next meeting in two weeks. Finding new ways to support their relationship with their father may affect their whole lives for years to come."

Sara just said, "Uh huh." She seemed in a daze. "I'll think about it."

The next week, Brad met with the children and with the Parent-Child Counselor. He explained to the children how feelings are contagious and that he was sorry that he upset them when he got angry with Tommy about his homework.

Brad: "There's other, better ways for me to teach you how important your homework is, like explaining to you that it will help you succeed in life, and that we're always learning. Like I'm learning to be more flexible in my thinking, and I want to teach you to be flexible too. Do you know what flexible means?"

Tommy replied: "Do you mean like when a piece of wood is real thin, it's real flexible, but when a piece of wood is real thick, it isn't?"

"Yes, Tommy," Brad replied. "That's it exactly. We have to learn to bend a little - without breaking.

The next thing to learn is to manage your own emotions. Like if you're real upset, to go to your room or to tell yourself encouraging things to help you calm down."

"Can I ask them a question?" Brad asked Mr. Desjardins.

Mr. Desjardins: "I'd like to stick to the workbook for now. After the session, you can tell me the question, then we can decide together whether or not it's a good question to bring up at the next session when they'll be letting you know some of their concerns."

After the session, Brad and Mr. Desjardins discussed Brad's question.

"That's a good question," the counselor said. "Of course, whenever you ask children a question like this, you have to be ready for any answer without getting angry at the answer. Otherwise, you won't know if they are just trying to please you. So you're sure any answer is okay with you?"

"Yes," Brad replied. "I just want to know."

At their next Parent-Child session, after Brad heard from the children what their concerns were, he asked his question.

Brad: "Tommy, do you still want to do woodworking projects with me?" Brad asked. "Do you feel upset when I ask if you want to build something? It's okay if you don't want to. I just want to know."

Tommy: "I really like building things with you, Dad. It's the fun-est thing we do. And my friend wants to build a boat. Can you help us with that?"

"Of course I'll help you," Brad smiled. "He can come over and I can help you both with it. But your mother said that you didn't want to do projects with me. Like when I asked if you wanted to build the birdhouse a few weeks ago."

Tommy: "Oh, I was just angry with you because you made mom cry."

"Well, that's ridiculous!" Brad replied, showing obvious irritation. "She makes herself cry. She does that a lot."

The counselor interrupted: "Slow down a minute, Brad. This is an important point. No one else can make someone else have feelings, although they might influence another person's feelings. It's real helpful for your son to feel comfortable to say what he thinks and feels to you. It's really good you just had this discussion. Tell Tommy you're glad he could be this open with you. You seem to have a great relationship."

"Thanks for telling me this Tommy," Brad replied. "I really appreciate you telling me everything, even if you think I won't like it. And I'm glad you still like woodworking projects, because I really enjoy doing them with you and Tara. Right, Tara?"

"Right, Daddy," Tara said. "And my toy box is too full. I need another one."

"Maybe we can work on it soon when I get my workbench from the house, now that I have regular weekends with you both. Hopefully, soon, I can see you half the time. We go back to court in a few weeks."

"Oops! Brad," the counselor interrupted. "Remember, we don't talk about court with the kids. They shouldn't even know when you and their mother are speaking with the judge. That's just for the grownups."

"Yeah, Dad," Tommy said. "We don't want you going to court and fighting with Mom. Please don't fight with her anymore."

"Did your mother tell you to say that?" Brad demanded. "I can't believe this double standard, that I'm supposed to keep quiet while she discusses everything with the children."

"Hold on, Brad," Mr. Desjardins said. "I appreciate your concern. I am also working with their mother to keep the court process away from the children. It's not easy for either of you, or anyone else. This is one of the hardest things in a divorce."

"But I have my rights as a father," Brad declared. "I should just have the kids half the time, and that should be the end of it. She's the one who's keeping it going in court by trying to eliminate me from the kids' lives."

"Mom didn't tell us to say that, Dad," Tommy suddenly interrupted. "We know she doesn't want us to see you, and we told her we want to see you. Didn't we, Tara?"

"Yeah. We want to see you," Tara said.

"So please stop fighting and talking about your rights, Dad," Tommy insisted. "Let's just see you like we do now and stop fighting for more."

"Yeah," said Tara.

"Let me jump in at this point and bring this part of the discussion to a close," the counselor said. "Do you want to thank your children for telling you their concerns today, Brad?"

"Oh, yes," said Brad. "Hearing what you have to say is very important to me, even if I don't always agree. I will think about what you said."

Mr. Desjardins replied: "I think you all are doing a good job at communicating and trying to protect your children. Progress is often slow with these big changes, but you are all to be congratulated on working on them. I can tell that you have a wonderful family, even if you live at two different houses now."

Sara's Lawyer Discusses Settlement [Step 4]

After Brad and Sara each had two sessions with the Parent-Child Counselor, Sara's lawyer scheduled a meeting to discuss the Family Court Mediation that would follow their third sessions.

"I got a phone call from your husband," Mr. Benjamin said, after Sara sat down in his office. "He said that he will drop his request for 50-50 parenting, if you will agree to one additional night than he currently has with his alternate weekend and Wednesdays overnight. He says he wants to work on a project with Tommy and one of his friends, and that Tommy told him he still enjoys their woodworking projects."

"But that's absurd!" Sara exclaimed. "I don't even want him to see the children. I think he's a monster, even if the judge doesn't see him that way. Look at how he upsets the children!"

Mr. Benjamin: "Brad authorized me to speak to the Parent-Child Counselor, so let's see what he thinks before we respond to Brad's proposal. Okay?"

"Don't bother," Sara sighed. "I already know what he thinks. He's trying to help me be flexible and moderate by sharing parenting with Brad. He doesn't think either of us is a bad parent. Can't you just get declarations and depositions from all the people who think that I'm the best parent and that Brad is the abusive, irresponsible parent?"

Mr. Benjamin: "All the declarations and depositions about the past won't help, if the Parent-Child Counselor says Brad is doing well in the present. The judge wants you both to learn new ways of being good parents, so what you each learn now is more important than proving that Brad used to be a jerk. Judges are getting tired of hearing that stuff anymore."

"So, I think you have to decide if you want to add another night to Brad's current schedule, or risk having the judge decide to give you both 50-50."

"Well, what if we just added one more evening every other week, but not an overnight?" Sara reluctantly asked.

"That's a good idea," he replied. "You can propose that to Brad in your mediation session. That sounds like flexible thinking to me."

A few days later, Sara called Mr. Benjamin after the mediation.

"We reached an agreement. Brad proposed an additional overnight every week. I proposed an additional evening every other week. We finally agreed to an additional evening every week, but not overnight."

Mr. Benjamin: "Excellent. This is much better than going to court. It will be easier to deal with each other and you'll save money. Did you discuss using a Parenting Coordinator in the future?"

"Oh yes. We agreed to use a Parenting Coordinator to resolve future disputes. And I'm sure there will be future disputes."

"Very good."

In the event that they did not reach an agreement in mediation or negotiations, then they would proceed to court to have the judge make decisions in Step 4. The following is how it may have gone.

Court Hearing —[Step 4]

Judge Clements: "Next case: Brad and Sara Turell. Please state your appearances."

Mr. Benjamin: "Your Honor, William Benjamin, for Sara Turell, who is present."

Ms. Skillin: "Shawn Skillin appearing on behalf of Brad Turell, your honor, who is present."

Judge Clements: "Are there any agreements by the parents?"

Mr. Benjamin: "No, your honor."

Ms. Skillin: "No, your honor."

Judge Clements: "That's disappointing. But let me explain how this hearing will go. First,

I'm going to ask some questions of your clients. Do I have your permission to question your client, Ms. Skillin?"

Ms. Skillin: "Yes, your honor."

Judge Clements: "Then, do I have your permission to ask some questions of your client, Mr. Benjamin?"

Mr. Benjamin: "Yes, your honor."

Judge Clements: "Thank you both. I'm going to ask each of you, Mr. Turell and Ms. Turell, to tell me what you have learned from your counseling. Then, I'm going to give you a future parenting scenario and ask how would deal with it using your skills. Then, I'm going to give you both a tentative decision in this matter. Then, you will have a chance to discuss my tentative decision in the hallway with your attorneys and each other, so that you can make serious efforts to resolve this case.

"If you have not reached an agreement, I will be very disappointed. But I will then hear your testimony and evidence and I will probably hear testimony from your Parent-Child Counselor, Mr. Desjardins, who will not make a recommendation, but who will tell me what he observed about each of your parenting skills.

"Then, I will make my long-term orders. Do you have any questions?

"Remember, when you ask me, a stranger, to make your decisions for you about your children, one or both of you will be disappointed. So keep in mind how important it is to try to reach an agreement today, if possible.

. . . .

[Sara is on the witness stand, which means that they failed to reach an agreement]:

Mr. Benjamin: "Please describe how the children reacted when their father knocked so hard on the door that the screen door fell off?"

Sara: "They were terrified that he might come in and kill us all! We were all afraid! They're still terrified to be around their father. They don't want to see him."

. . . .

Brad is on the witness stand]:

Ms. Skillin: "Please describe how the children react to you when they have visitation with you on the weekends."

Brad: "They have a wonderful time. They love doing projects with me. We laugh and play and get along really great."

Ms. Skillin: "How do you deal with it when you feel angry with them?"

Brad: "First, I tell them I'm going to take a break for a few minutes. Then I calm myself down, by reminding myself that they're good kids and I'm a good parent. Then I think of a moderate behavior I can use in the situation, like telling them we can't have dinner until they finish cleaning up or doing their homework, whatever it is. And I try to plan ahead, so problems don't come up too often anyway."

. . . .

[Mr. Desjardins, the Parent-Child Counselor is on the witness stand. This means that the parents signed releases to allow him to share observations during the counseling.]:

Judge Clements: "I really appreciate your observations of the parents, and how well they appear to be doing in their counseling with their children. Now, do the children seem afraid of spending time with their father?"

Mr. Desjardins: "No. In fact, they seem quite comfortable with him. After a few minutes, I have observed them relaxing and opening up with him. I have observed them telling him what they like and what they don't like about how he spends time with them. They told him they don't want him to fight about the parenting schedule with their mother."

Judge Clements: "And how did he respond to these concerns of the children?"

Mr. Desjardins: "He struggled for a moment, looking like he might get angry, then he thanked the children for telling him that and said he would think about it."

Judge Clements: "And how did the mother respond to the children when they had negative things to say to her?"

Mr. Desjardins: "She also started to get angry, but then caught herself and told the children her feelings were her responsibility and not the kids' responsibility."

Judge Clements: "So, would you say that both parents are trying to 'check themselves,' to respond moderately with the children even when they're getting upset?"

Mr. Desjardins: "Yes."

Judge Clements: "And do you have any concerns about the children spending substantial time with either parent now?"

Mr. Desjardins: "No."

Judge Clements: "Thank you, Mr. Desjardins, for your observations. I will consider them in making my findings and orders."

Comment: This example includes the steps described in the TIMELINE in Chapter One. However, many cases may not have as many steps, such as doing without an interim hearing between Steps 2 and 3. Any mediation should occur after both Steps 2 and 3 have occurred. If they reach a settlement in mediation, negotiations with lawyers, or other method, then there is no need for the last court hearing. Early feedback indicates that many potentially high-conflict cases do not return to court for hearings, after New Ways has been initially ordered or agreed by stipulation.

CHAPTER 4
Step 1: Getting Started

Ordering or Agreeing to the New Ways Method   [Step 1A]

New Ways for Families can be ordered by the court as soon as the parents enter the court system, especially when there is a request for restricted parenting orders or other indicator that a high-conflict case may arise. However, parents can easily stipulate (agree) to participate in this method without needing a court hearing. It can be part of a Collaborative Divorce, a Divorce Mediation, or a negotiated divorce with or without lawyers. This 4-Step method can also occur after a divorce, especially if a high level of parent conflict continues to exist.

High-conflict court cases (pre and post divorce) often begin with an emergency hearing for protective orders, at the request of one parent without the other parent present. New Ways for Families can be ordered at the first full hearing with both parties in attendance (or at least given notice). Both parents are ordered to participate, so that both parents will learn the same skills and teach the children the same skills.

If necessary, concurrent orders can be made at this initial full hearing, including temporary protective/restraining orders and restricted parenting plans. (See example in Chapter Three.) Then, after Steps 2 and 3 of New Ways for Families has been completed (after a total of approximately 12 weeks), if the parents are unable to reach a settlement on their parenting plans and must return to court, then the court will quiz the parents on their new skills and make comprehensive, ongoing orders for the family (Step 4). The court should schedule a hearing date for Step 4, as a motivation for parents to complete Steps 2 and 3 before that date. Without such a date, counseling orders are often ignored or sabotaged by one or both parents.

See <u>Appendix I</u> for a Sample court order for New Ways for Families.

The information to put in the Order should be approximately as follows:

<u>Findings</u>: If the parties agree, then no Findings are necessary. If the parties do not agree to participate in counseling, the court can order it over objection in many states. In California, under Family Code Section 3190, the court must make these two findings.

> #1: The dispute between the parents will certainly qualify if "the parents requests are strongly opposing," "there are reports of abuse or alienation," and/or "one parent is requesting restricted parenting for the other."

> #2: With sliding fee scale, the counseling is within most parent's ability.

Orders: here are recommendations for the blanks on the Sample Court Order, based on the date the order is issued as "Day 1":

#1. Contact Individual Parent Counselor:	_____	[7 days after Day 1]
#4. Individual Counseling completed by:	_____	[7 weeks after Day 1]
#5. Interim Hearing Date (if needed, see above)	_____	[8 weeks after Day 1]
#10. Parent-Child Counseling completed by:	_____	[13 weeks after Day 1]
#12. Court mediation completed by:	_____	[14 weeks after Day 1]
#13. Next court hearing on:	_____	[18 weeks after Day 1]

The above is a very structured timeline. It is the opposite of family court as usual, but what potentially high-conflict parents need. By providing parents a very clear structure in New Ways, and by having both parents follow the same schedule, they will either be motivated for success or will demonstrate to the court who is able and who is not. Our experience is that most parents are very motivated at the beginning of this process and appreciate knowing exactly what to do when.

If counseling appointments are delayed because of illness, travel, counselor unavailability, or other reasons, there can be two appointments in a week to make them up. Both parents should stay on the same schedule, as it is a parallel process throughout. If one parent is unable to follow such a structure, their ability to follow a parenting schedule may also be in question. Such information will be helpful to the court.

Selecting Individual Parent Counselors   [Step 1B]

Each parent should select his or her own Individual Parent Counselor within 7 days of the initial court order, drawn from a list of licensed mental health professionals trained in the New Ways for Families method, or as assigned by the counseling agency providing the service. Such lists may be provided by the court, attorneys or mental health professionals in the county.

If working with a private therapist instead of a counseling agency, each parent makes their own arrangements with the counselor, including scheduling, negotiating fees, and routine paperwork. They should start as soon as possible, so that the counseling can be completed by the deadlines in the court order (see above).

Preparing Behavioral Declarations [Step 1C]

The focus of New Ways for Families is on learning positive future behavior, rather than criticizing or defending each other's past behavior. While the court may need to make findings regarding past negative behavior, the emphasis should be on encouraging the learning of new skills in Steps 2 and 3.

To this end, each party (with his or her lawyer, if any) should prepare a Behavioral Declaration and Reply Behavioral Declaration, which will be provided to all three of the New Ways counselors by the following schedule:

Behavioral Declaration Due Dates

To own counselor by:	2 business days before own counseling begins
To other parent by:	Same date as above
To Parent-Child Counselor:	10 calendar days before first Parent-Child session

Reply Behavioral Declaration/Affidavit Due Dates

To other parent by:	5 business days after receiving other's Declaration
To own counselor by:	Same date as above
To Parent-Child Counselor:	10 calendar days before first Parent-Child session

The Behavioral Declarations focus narrowly on the three most concerning behaviors of the other parent, described in as neutral terms as possible to help the parents focus on changing these specific behaviors without having to defend their past behaviors. Each parent will also prepare a Reply Behavioral Declaration, indicating whether he or she 1) agrees that the concerning negative behavior occurred, 2) does not agree that the concerning behavior occurred or occurred that way, and 3) explaining behaviors he or she is considering changing.

In the event that parents volunteer for New Ways, rather than being ordered by the court, they should still prepare Behavioral Declarations to assist their counselors and lawyers in supporting specific behavior changes. See Appendix II for sample Behavioral Declarations.

Lawyer Assistance

New Ways for Families provides lawyers with a unique opportunity to emphasize client counseling, while keeping the door open to litigation. The structure of this method supports the attorney's efforts at client counseling, through the preparation of the Behavioral

Declaration at the beginning of the process and by delaying litigation while the client goes through Individual Parent Counseling (Step 2) and Parent-Child Counseling (Step 3). The decision of whether to negotiate or litigate should be made only after these efforts at behavior change have been made. This reduces the likelihood of high-conflict litigation.

As described in Chapter Three, the court and New Ways counselors need behavioral information to make decisions and teach new skills. Preparing the Behavioral Declaration helps the lawyer calm down a high-conflict client (or an anxious client whose spouse is high conflict) and focuses them on productive behavior change – both the other parent's and their own.

Domestic violence, child abuse, child alienation, substance abuse and false allegations are the most common issues in high-conflict cases. The goal of the Behavioral Declarations is to identify the most concerning behaviors and whether there is a pattern to these behaviors. Depending on the court system, the court may use these declarations in making decisions, although the parties could also file any other documents they would ordinarily provide to the court. A court system may decide not to use these in court. They are not necessary to the court process, but may be helpful to the court in understanding the parties' concerns in brief. An attorney may request that these declarations be used at court or not used at court. The primary purpose of these declarations is to provide a basic overview of the case to the counselors; therefore, attorneys are discouraged from filing these with the court.

The New Ways counselors will receive copies of both parties' Behavioral Declarations to assist their clients in focusing on necessary issues during counseling. However, the New Ways Counselors would only see the parents' Behavioral Declarations, Reply Behavioral Declarations and the court's order. They would not see any other documents, in order to keep them removed from the court process and help the client focus on future behavior rather than recounting the past.

Examples of both parents' Behavioral Declarations and Reply Behavioral Declarations from the case described in Chapter Three are located in Appendix II. In the examples, one party has an attorney and the other is self-representing. If both parties are self-representing, they should still prepare these same declarations.

Content

Each parent's Behavioral Declaration should be 2 pages, with three parts. For example:

Mother's [Father's] 3 Strongest Concerns About Father's Parenting

Mother's View of Father's 3 Best Strengths

Mother's Parenting Requests

Behavioral Declarations are very brief and focused on parent behavior. The three most concerning behaviors would be explained in one paragraph each, in as neutral, descriptive terms as possible. Parents are encouraged to focus on the WHO, WHAT, WHEN and WHERE of the most concerning behavior, including whether there is a pattern of this behavior or not.

By focusing on behavior, rather than on the "all-good" or "all-bad" quality of the person as a whole, this process will help both parents think about behavior change. In high-conflict cases, parents often see themselves in all-or-nothing terms. Comments often focus on the whole person, such as: "He has only himself to blame." "She never has anything good to say." "I have done nothing wrong." Behavior is a better focus.

In the Behavioral Declaration, positive qualities of each parent are also mentioned. Research shows that positive behavior change is built more easily on success rather than failure. Requiring each parent to validate the other's positive qualities helps both parents support each other's behavior change, which benefits their children in the long run.

Reply Behavioral Declarations

The Reply Behavioral Declarations have two parts. For example:

Father's Agreement/Disagreement with Mother's Concerns

Father's Revised Parenting Requests (If Any)

The purpose of the Reply Behavioral Declarations is for each parent to briefly say whether they Agree or Disagree with the concerns of the other parent. This lets the court easily determine whether there is a dispute over the existence of a behavior problem, or just an issue of what should be done. Parents are encouraged to acknowledge past inappropriate behavior, so that the focus can be on behavior change for the future.

All professionals should reinforce this focus on the future. However, lawyers in particular will be involved in re-training their clients to think and speak in terms of future behavior. It is often the lawyer who trains the client in appropriate court strategies and behavior more than anyone else.

CHAPTER 5
Step 2: Individual Parent Counseling

In this initial step, each parent meets with a separate individual counselor. This individual counseling is confidential. Each parent meets with his or her counselor for 6 one-hour sessions, over a period of six weeks. This counselor's job is solely to assist the client in learning new ways of flexible thinking, managed emotions, practicing moderate behaviors, and checking yourself during the separation or divorce process. The New Ways Counselor does not report to courts, lawyers, or other professionals involved in a contested case. Instead, each parent reports back what has been learned to the court or other appropriate professional. The burden is on the parent to learn and practice these skills in the counseling.

General Principles for Individual Parent Counselors

Parents in families with child abuse and child alienation, or high risk for abuse or alienation, appear to have 3 specific common characteristics:

High-conflict thinking (all-or-nothing solutions, jumping to conclusions, etc.)

Unmanaged emotions with children (including yelling, crying, blaming, etc.)

Extreme behaviors with children (hitting, impulsive decisions, inability to control anger at exchanges, frequent negative comments about others, competition with other parent over personal qualities, exposing children to adult discussions and arguments, excessive expectations of intimacy with child, etc.)

When these parents enter the family court system, the stress of the adversarial process often increases their anxiety, which increases these negative characteristics. Because of their high-conflict thinking and lack of boundaries with their children, their children often adopt similar high-conflict thinking and lack of emotional boundaries with the dysfunctional parent(s).

When their parents engage in all-or-nothing thinking ("It's all your father's fault." "Your mother is unfit to raise you." "You're on my side or you're against me." etc.), their children often show alienation from one parent and an extreme alignment with the other parent. This appears to occur independently of whether or not there is child abuse. It appears to be more related to the above on-going general characteristics (with thousands of little incidents, mostly unconscious) than to one incident of abuse or one inappropriate comment. The issue is the on-going influence of the above characteristics and how each parent communicates them.

Therefore, the focus of this individual counseling is teaching the four basic skills: flexible thinking, managed emotions, using moderate behaviors and checking yourself (to use these skills when new issues arise). However, the importance of the individual counseling is for the counselor to work on client resistance to learning these skills. Many high-conflict people are "high conflict" because they lack self-awareness and the current ability to change their behavior for success in different environments. The therapist's job is to try to help the client become aware of resistance to change and learn to manage it as an ordinary part of adult life. This is addressed as managing "hurdles" throughout New Ways for Families.

In many ways, the benefit of having individual counseling in these cases is to build a connection between the individual therapist and the client. Avoid criticizing the client (which builds resistance) or agreeing with the client (which builds resistance to change). Attention should be paid to using empathy, attention and respect to build a relationship and assist learning and growth, which is the foundation that many high-conflict people have been lacking, which makes it harder for them to learn.

The Parent Workbook will help guide the Individual Parent Counseling. Efforts have been made to have it address each of the skills with increasing complexity. The articles at the end of the Workbook have been helpful in teaching negotiation skills and responding to hostile communications. These skills will assist the client in making decisions with (or without) contact with the child's other parent.

Last Session Jointly with Both Parents

The last session of New Ways Individual Counseling may include both parents together, if it appears that this would be productive. The subject matter is ways to recognize and support the other parent's relationship with the child/ren. In extremely high-conflict cases, this would be kept separate. However, in some cases this could be a major stepping stone toward a less-conflictual parenting relationship.

Therefore, in the fifth session you will need to address whether the sixth session will be held jointly with both parties and both therapists, or will be held as the final individual session. If the parents are able to meet together and discuss their new ways of communicating and making decisions, it should relieve a lot of pressure on the children. However, in more extreme cases, any contact directly between the parents may not be realistic, and New Ways for Families is designed to keep the parents separate from each other, if necessary.

Confidentiality

Since the Individual Parent Counseling is confidential, it is very important to resist requests from the clients to write a letter or declaration for the court. Just gently explain this rule and return them to the subject at hand. Encourage them to use the counseling to build tools and strength for dealing with their children and others themselves.

Parent Workbook

An essential part of the individual counseling process is the Parent Workbook. The first section of the Workbook is to be completed during the Individual Counseling sessions, while the second section is to be completed during the Parent-Child Counseling sessions. This workbook helps each parent and his or her counselor focus most effectively on learning key skills in a short period of time. This Workbook is designed to help the client and counselor work together toward the client's goals, but not to limit their discussions while working on these goals. Instead, the Workbook provides a simple way of beginning discussions and reinforcing what the client is learning. Counselors may use different styles and methods while working through this Workbook. The Workbook helps the client develop self-help skills and makes the New Ways for Families method predictable. The Individual Parent Counseling section of the Parent Workbook remains confidential with the individual counselor, unless the client wishes to handle it otherwise. It is up to the client's sole discretion.

The counselor should provide the Parent Workbook to the client at the first session or before the first session. Clients can also obtain them from **www.NewWays4Families. com.** They need to have a Workbook at the first session, or this method cannot work. It is helpful for the counselor to have a copy of the Workbook for his or her own use, and to be thoroughly familiar with each session before it begins.

CHAPTER 6
Step 3: Parent-Child Counseling

Instead of using an individual counselor for the child, New Ways for Families focuses directly on assisting parent-child relationships with a New Ways Parent-Child Counselor. Each parent will meet with the child/ren 3 times. The parents will alternate weeks for these sessions with the same Parent-Child Counselor (who is a different person from the two individual parent counselors in Step 1). These sessions may last 1-2 hours, depending on the age of the child/ren and the extent of the need for the counselor to have separate discussions with a parent or child.

Each of the 3 sessions has a different focus. In the first parent-child session, the parent teaches the child/ren the basic lessons he or she has learned about flexible thinking, managed emotions, practicing moderate behaviors and checking yourself. The Parent-Child Counselor supports and assists the parent and child/ren in thinking of examples of each of these lessons. The other parent's first session covers these same lessons from the other parent's perspective, thereby reinforcing the lessons and that both parents support the child/ren in learning these lessons.

The second session focuses on the parent hearing the child/ren's concerns in the separation or divorce process. The parent mostly listens and acknowledges what the child/ren are saying, without discussing parenting schedules or negotiating with the child/ren.

The third session focuses on parents and child/ren practicing new behaviors together. If appropriate, this session would include both parents together with the child/ren. If the parents have concurrently negotiated changes in their parenting schedule (with their attorneys, a mediator, or other professionals), methods of communication and decision-making, then they would jointly explain these changes to the child/ren and discuss the new behaviors for all involved.

Parent Workbook

The Parent-Child Counseling section of the Parent Workbook structures each of these three sessions. The parent should be prepared to speak to the child in the manner structured by the Workbook, and the therapist should be prepared to assist the parent with this.

During the parent-child sessions, the parent will write in the Workbook. This provides structure for their discussions and consistency between the lessons both parents are teaching in their separate sessions. The workbook is simple so that it is a starting point for discussions rather than a distraction from important parent-child communication.

Please read the Workbook thoroughly before each session, as each session is very different and has different goals.

No Confidentiality

The Parent-Child Counseling is not confidential. The counselor can be called to testify at court to answer questions about the parents' interactions with their child/ren, to assist the judge in making difficult decisions about parenting plans and future treatment. Similarly, this section of the Parent Workbook is also non-confidential.

However, the Parent-Child Counselor would not write a report or make verbal recommendations, other than specific parenting suggestions to the parents. This keeps the emphasis on the counselor helping the parents learn skills to assist in their parenting and making their own decisions, rather than drawing the Counselor into a primarily decision-making role.

The Parent-Child Counselor can also be available for future sessions between the parent(s) and child, if the parents make future requests or the court orders future parent-child counseling.

CHAPTER 7
Step 4: Family (Or Court) Decision-Making

After the parents have completed Step 2 (Individual Parent Counseling) and Step 3 (Parent-Child Counseling), Step 4 focuses on decision-making. There are two basic options:

Negotiation of Parenting Plan in New Ways for Families

In the structure of New Ways for Families, the ideal time to negotiate a parenting plan with the parties is between the 2nd and 3rd Parent-Child Counseling sessions. At each parent's 2nd session with the children, they will have heard some of the children's concerns about the separation or divorce. This session has the potential to increase empathy for the children and to decrease the parents' desire to litigate their future.

Of course, some high-conflict parents will not be able to empathize with their children no matter what they do, but it is worth at least one attempt to negotiate a complete parenting plan with them at this time. If they are successful, or even partially successful, at reaching agreements on their parenting, then they can separately or jointly explain their agreements to the children during their 3rd Parent-Child Counseling session. This could include agreements about the parenting schedule, how they will communicate, and how future decisions will get made.

The negotiations could be conducted by lawyers for both parties in a 4-way joint conference with both parents. This gives the lawyers opportunity to go back and forth, meeting jointly and separately with their clients to discuss realistic options. High-conflict clients especially need lots of separate attention, realistic education and reassurance throughout the negotiation process.

An alternative would be for the parties to go to mediation. They could meet with a family court mediator or a private mediator. In California, the courts require a mental health professional's recommendation before the judge can make parenting orders (except that temporary orders can be made).

Lawyers could meet with their clients beforehand to thoroughly discuss the difference between realistic and unrealistic options. One of the biggest problems for high-conflict parties is having unrealistic expectations throughout the legal process.

Since the parents will have both been trained in flexible thinking, managed emotions, and moderate behaviors during their counseling, attorneys can remind them of these skills when their negotiations get difficult or the parents lock into rigid positions, thereby reminding parents to "check yourself" when dealing with new issues.

If they are unsuccessful at reaching an out-of-court settlement, counsel can explain the pros and cons of the options ahead in court.

Litigation of Parenting Plan in New Ways for Families

Since decision-making is Step 4 of *New Ways for Families*, and since the parents were unable to use their skills to reach their own agreements, the court should start out by asking each parent to explain what he or she has learned while in Step 1 and Step 2 of *New Ways for Families*. Then, the court should quiz each parent about hypothetical parenting scenarios that are slight variations of the concerning behaviors raised in each other's court pleadings.

Then, the court may proceed with a normal hearing or trial on parenting matters, with testimony and other evidence. It is expected that there will be a contrast for each parent between their statements about what they have learned and their litigation behavior and requests.

For example, a parent may state that he or she has learned to avoid all-or-nothing thinking, but then request an all-or-nothing parenting plan (such as no contact) with no reasonable basis. Or a parent may suddenly become extremely emotional and appear unable to manage their feelings. Such inconsistencies between their statements and their behavior will help the court in making parenting decisions for them.

In *New Ways for Families*, the Parent-Child Counselor is not confidential and is available to give testimony to the court. However, he or she does not write a report, which keeps the adversarial posturing of the parties to a minimum during the Parent-Child Counseling and avoids the over-reactions that parents often have about particular words or phrases used to describe them in written reports.

Instead, he or she can give testimony and answer the court's questions about his or her observations of the parents' interactions with their children. In many ways, this is much more informative than hearing evidence and argument about past behaviors which no one else observed except the parties or potentially biased witnesses.

Requested orders can still include the full range of options, including: parenting classes, more counseling, drug treatment, batterers treatment, anger management, restraining orders, supervised visitation, and very limited parenting time. It is expected that the appropriate level of treatment and/or restrictions will be clearer after Steps 2, 3 and 4.

Assessment by the Court

After hearing what the parties have learned, after quizzing them on their responses to hypothetical scenarios (similar to those described in their court pleadings), the court will have a better idea of which parent(s) has the demonstrated ability to reflect on their own behavior and to make changes. The court might wish to consider the following basic categories each parent fits into regarding behavior and behavior change (observations by the Parent-Child Counselor may be necessary to assist with this):

Category 1: Generally appropriate parenting skills, with no significant problems.

Category 2: Problems in parenting, but able to make significant changes.

Category 3: Problems in parenting, and unable to make significant changes.

Category 4: Unable to determine, so additional assessment may be necessary.

The result of the above determination will help the court in making decisions regarding future treatment, if any, and future parenting restrictions, if any. For example, based on each of the above categories:

Category 1: Court would order no further treatment and no restrictions on parenting.

Category 2: Court would order further treatment and further restricted parenting, but with a review hearing in 1, 3, 6 or 12 months, whichever is appropriate for the case.

Category 3: Court would order no further treatment and order long-term restricted parenting, perhaps with a Parenting Coordinator.

Category 4: The court would order a custody/psychological evaluation and/or the appointment of a lawyer for the child/ren (Guardian ad litem or Minor's Counsel) to represent the child/ren's interests in further court hearings.

At this hearing or a subsequent hearing, based on the evidence before the court, the court could also order drug treatment, batterer's treatment, more counseling, and/or parenting classes. A future review hearing could be ordered.

Once these orders are made, the court could order the appointment of a Parenting Co-ordinator to handle future disputes between the parties over the implementation of their parenting schedule.

CHAPTER 8
Decision Skills Class

The *New Ways for Families* **class model** is not a parenting class itself. It focuses on more basic conflict resolution skills. However, the *New Ways for Families* Decision Skills Class sessions can be inserted into any existing parenting class curriculum, or the three sessions can be taught as a 60-90 minute class each. Class instructors are required to follow the Instructor's Manual and may take an optional 3-hour training provided by High Conflict Institute. See Chapter Seventeen for Training options.

The New Ways class instructor applies the three sessions using the Decision Skills Workbook, involving the parents in writing assignments and practice exercises as a group.

Structure

The classes focus on four key skills for decision making, similar to, but briefer than, the exercises in the Parent Workbook and the Collaborative Workbook. Parents may read the class session materials before or during the class, but are expected to do the exercises during the class as a group so they can then be discussed as a group. All exercises and discussions are focused on the skills and hypothetical cases, as the parents should not discuss their own cases during this skills-focused class (this is especially important with potentially high-conflict parents who have a hard time not discussing their own cases).

The classes are structured as follows:

Class 1:   Communicating with B.I.F.F. responses

This class teaches a simple technique for written responses to hostile communications, such as emails, that are Brief, Informative, Friendly, and Firm.

Two practice exercises followed by group discussion.

Class 2:   <u>Calm Yourself with Encouraging Statements</u>

This class teaches a simple method of writing and memorizing positive statements about the parent's strengths and areas of learning new skills.

Two practice exercises followed by group discussion.

Class 3:   <u>Making Proposals</u>

This class teaches a simple method of turning complaints about the past into proposals for the future, including the Who, What, When, and Where of a proposal. It also teaches parents how to respond to proposals by asking constructive questions and saying: Yes. No. or I'll think about it.

Two practice exercises followed by group discussion

<u>Checking Yourself</u>

This class also teaches "Checking Yourself," which is important so that the parent focuses on their own behavior more than on the other parent's behavior, and reminds him or herself to use these skills whenever decisions need to be made.

One exercise followed by group discussion.

How the Decision Skills Class is Different than a Parenting Class

The Decisions Skills Class is not designed to replace a parenting class. General parenting classes are beneficial for most parents. However, many high-conflict parents often have personality disorders, or traits thereof, requiring a different approach by professionals.

Treatments for personality disorders have shown that many high-conflict parents may be able to change, with sufficient structure and learning small skills in small steps. Instead of focusing on practical skills for conflict resolution, parenting classes often focus on providing education and resources in a lecture format, as if they are speaking to a reasonable person. They assume that parents will hear the information, process it, and change their behavior accordingly.

However, with high-conflict people, the parenting class instructors are "talking to the wrong brain." High-conflict parents are unable to take in the information and change their behavior accordingly because they are "stuck" making decisions based on their feelings — not logic. They view the world through their right, emotional side of the brain, rather than the left, logical side. Therefore, high-conflict parents don't really "hear" the information presented in parenting classes because they don't automatically engage the logical side of their brain. Some parenting classes do require participation, often in small group exercises. However, without more structure and repetition, high-conflict parents don't learn from these exercises.

CHAPTER 9
Collaborative Divorce And New Ways

New Ways for Families **may be helpful for any family** involved in Collaborative Divorce, and especially helpful for potentially high-conflict families. New Ways is very compatible with the philosophy and structure of Collaborative Divorce, as it teaches the use of the four key conflict-reducing skills of flexible thinking, managed emotions, moderate behaviors and checking yourself (to use these skills when new issues arise). It will benefit families who are at risk of dropping out of Collaborative Divorce, or who get stuck in the process at various points because they have insufficient experience or practice with using these skills.

Ideally, New Ways will be implemented early in the collaborative process, so that parents can use their skills throughout the process for easier communication and decision-making. As more families use collaborative divorce, the need for – and opportunity for – methods of handling high-conflict families in collaborative will grow.

In many ways, New Ways will be more successful in the Collaborative model than in the Court-Based model, because parents already start out agreeing to collaborate rather than having to be ordered to cooperate with each other by the court. For this reason, the New Ways process in collaborative is shorter, more flexible and has fewer of the boundaries used in the Court-Based model to block high-conflict behavior.

Collaborative professionals are encouraged to read Chapter One of this Professional Guidebook, then Chapters Nine and the remaining chapters. There is no need for collaborative professionals to read Chapters Two through Eight, as they are focused on the Court-Based and Class models. However, since many collaborative professionals also work with family court cases (lawyers, mental health professionals, financial specialists), there is one Professional Guidebook for both Court-Based cases and Collaborative cases.

Differences Between Collaborative & Court-Based Models

The main differences between the New Ways Collaborative model compared to the New Ways Court-Based model are:

1. **Coaching Format:** The four skills are taught in a brief (3-session) Coaching format, rather than in six Individual Parent Counseling sessions. Rather than focusing on overcoming resistance to using the four skills, the coaching format emphasizes briefly practicing the four skills in making proposals, responding to hostile emails, etc. Since Coaches are not acting as therapists, this avoids the intensity of a counseling relationship. If a client(s) needs more, he or she can be referred to an outside therapist who can continue with the client after the collaborative process is over, if needed or desired.

2. **Non-Confidential:** In the Collaborative model, the New Ways coaching sessions are non-confidential within the team, in keeping with the whole collaborative approach. All team members, including the coach(es), can talk with each other for the clients' benefit. This makes New Ways much easier, in regard to scheduling coaching sessions and Child Specialist meetings. Also, the collaborative team can discuss ways to reinforce both parents in their use of these skills, and jointly help the parents overcome any barriers to using these skills.

3. **Child Specialist Role**: In the Court-Based model, the Parent-Child Counselor can testify in court about his or her observations of the parent-child interactions, and rarely has individual contact with a parent or a children, as their meetings are all with a parent and child together. In the Collaborative model, the Child Specialist meets with the parents and children at least three times to address the New Ways issues, but would never have any role with the court. Therefore, there is less risk of a high-conflict parent trying to influence the Child Specialist's opinion, so that the Child Specialist may meet separately any number of times with the children and parents, before, between and after the three New Ways meetings.

4. **Joint Sessions Both Parents**: In the New Ways Collaborative model, there is automatically a joint coaching session and one or more joint New Ways meetings with their Child Specialist. In the Court-Based model, the parents can choose to have no joint meetings at all, because of abuse or an extremely high level of mistrust.

5. **Workbooks**: In the New Ways Collaborative model, there is one workbook, with many fewer exercises than in the Court-Based model. This Collaborative Parent Workbook includes sections for the Coaching sessions and for the Child Specialist meetings.

6. **Timespan**: New Ways in Collaborative Divorce can occur in as short a period as

4-6 weeks, since there are only three New Ways coaching sessions, followed by three Child Specialist meetings. These sessions can occur once or twice a week, in order to help the parents move quickly into decision-making, if desired. On the other hand, these sessions can be spread out by agreement of the parties over a much longer period of weeks or months.

7. **Prevention**: In the Collaborative process, it is much easier to engage clients in New Ways for Families at the start of the case. In contrast, in the Court-Based model, parents are often ordered into New Ways after they have become "high conflict" and have a lot more resistance to changing their behavior. In Collaborative there is the opportunity to teach positive skills before anyone has "acted badly." Since the New Ways skills are very basic, they can help parents start off on a positive footing which can be maintained by the whole collaborative team throughout the process.

Basic Structure

New Ways for Families in Collaborative Divorce is structured to focus on skills first, then on decisions. Therefore, it is designed with the same 4 Steps as in the Court-Based model. Each step prepares parents for the next Step. However, in the Collaborative model, many of the tasks are different. For example, the parties already know their Coach(es) and their Child Specialist, so that they do not need to spend time on selecting them in using the *New Ways for Families* steps.

STEP 1: GETTING STARTED

Screening: There are several reasons that a family would be encouraged to agree to use the New Ways process in Collaborative Divorce, as early in the case as possible:

They have a significant dispute about parenting. For example, one parent believes that the other needs restricted parenting (supervised or very few hours).

It's hard to determine whether Collaborative Divorce is appropriate for a particular potentially high-conflict family. The clients could be asked to agree to use the New Ways method at the start of the case, to give them a better chance of success in the collaborative process. If they will not agree to use this short-term method of practicing skills before making big decisions, then they are unlikely to be able to collaborate in making their other decisions.

If either parent asks for it, after learning about *New Ways for Families*.

While it is currently designed for parents, the basic skills and coaching exercises of New Ways could be practiced by any potentially high-conflict couple, even if the issues are just financial and there are no children. However, they would just do the three sessions of Coaching, as there would be no need for Child Specialist meetings.

<u>Signing Agreement</u>: Both parents should sign the <u>Agreement to Use *New Ways for Families* in Collaborative Divorce</u>, which appears at the end of this Chapter. This way, they are both committed to completing the process and going through the steps of this process at approximately the same time.

<u>Scheduling Sessions</u>: Each parent should be responsible for scheduling their sessions with his or her Coach and the Child Specialist. In their Agreement above, they should have included end dates for each section of New Ways, which will help them both go through the process at the same pace.

<u>Obtaining Workbooks*</u>: Each parent should be responsible for obtaining their own <u>Collaborative Parent Workbook</u>, either from their Coach or from the New Ways website at **www.NewWays4Families.com**, prior to their first New Ways session with his or her coach.

Coaches should also obtain copies of the <u>Collaborative Parent Workbook</u> prior to the first session, so that they can discuss the material and exercises in depth.

*Make sure that you and your client obtains the <u>Collaborative Parent Workbook</u>, and not the "Parent Workbook" which is used in the <u>court-based</u> New Ways method.

<u>No Declarations</u>: In contrast to the Court-Based model of New Ways, in the Collaborative model there is no need for declarations to be provided to the Coach(es) or the Child Specialist. Since the New Ways process is non-confidential within the team, the Coach(es) and Child Specialist should already have a good background on the family and the most difficult issues which may arise.

STEP 2: NEW WAYS COACHING SESSIONS

In the Collaborative model of New Ways, there may be one coach who works with both parents, or a separate coach for each parent, depending on your local model and the needs of the parties. If it is a potentially high-conflict case, this author recommends two coaches, so that fierce perceived loyalty issues do not arise for a single coach. The following description can be used by one or two coaches.

> This step includes 3 Coaching sessions
>
> Two separate New Ways meetings with each parent and Coach
>
> Then, one joint New Ways meeting with both parents and Coach(es)

The focus of these sessions is strengthening and practicing four conflict-reducing skills: flexible thinking, managed emotions, moderate behaviors and checking yourself.

Flexibility

This method is designed to be flexible, so that parents and coaches can meet more often than the sessions described above, and can add issues beyond the skills in the Workbooks for discussion in separate or joint meetings. Essentially, you should collaborate in making any changes to this basic method, so that it works most effectively for you. However, it has been designed based on the author's many years of studying what doesn't work. So you are encouraged to use this process without reducing the number of meetings or exercises – just add to it when agreed upon by those involved.

Not Therapy

Collaborative Coaches are not acting as therapists. Therefore, New Ways in Collaborative Divorce is not designed to be therapy. If your client wishes to have therapy or you believe that your client needs to have some therapy, you should refer him or her to an outside therapist who uses the New Ways method in therapy (there are different workbooks for that) – or other therapy methods supportive of the collaborative process. (Watch out for therapists who support their client's negative viewpoint of the other party without question, or who believe their client is purely a victim who does not need to take responsibility for problem-solving, or who escalate their client's legal demands in a misguided effort to help their client be assertive.)

The benefit of an outside therapist is that your client can continue in therapy after the divorce decisions have been made. Coaches should focus on making decisions and their work should be finished once all the decisions have been made. Therefore, it is important that you do not attempt to open up deep emotional issues or "family-of-origin" issues while coaching your client in the New Ways skills and in making decisions in the Collaborative Process.

Using the Workbook

The <u>Collaborative Parent Workbook</u> is designed to provide information, topics for discussion and exercises to practice the skills. Both parents are expected to work on the same skills and the same exercises in their own Workbooks. Ideally, they will be working on these at the same time, so that they will be ready to meet with the Child Specialist to use these skills with their children at the same time.

Instructions for Coaches:

1. Before first New Ways Coaching Meeting

The Client should obtain the <u>Collaborative Parent Workbook</u> from their coach or from the website, **www.NewWays4Families.com**. Tell them to bring the workbook to the first coaching meeting about *New Ways for Families*. <u>Prior to the meeting</u>, if possible, the client should read the information for the first session (Session 1: Skills for Resilience and Flexible Thinking) and write Exercises #1 - #4. If they haven't read anything or done any exercises, just cover this during your session.

2. During the first New Ways Coaching Meeting

Explain the exercises to the client as much as possible, and discuss the material and exercises for Session 1. If the client hasn't done Exercises #1-#4, you can do them during the first coaching session, or have the client do them after the session.

Then, give instructions to read the material for Session 2 and do Exercises #5- #9 before your second meeting about New Ways.

With the written exercises, let the client know to just do the best he or she can.

This should be a successful experience, so there should be no negative feedback about not writing the exercises between sessions. If necessary, have the client do all of the writing exercises during your coaching sessions.

3. Second New Ways Coaching Meeting

Make sure you have read the materials and articles in the Collaborative Parent Workbook for Session 2 (Managed Emotions and Moderate Behaviors). Discuss the written exercises with your client and anything else that seems relevant to applying these skills successfully during the collaborative process.

Prepare for your third New Ways Coaching Meeting, which will be a joint meeting with the other parent (and coach). Discuss with your client how he or she can use these skills to make that meeting most successful and lay the groundwork for a future collaboration as parents.

4. Before Your Third New Ways Coaching Meeting

Have your client read the materials and write the exercises (#10-#12) for Session 3: Joint Coaching Session.

5. Third New Ways Coaching Meeting (Joint)

Guide the parents in sharing their written responses to the questions in Exercises #10 - #12, as you believe appropriate. You may focus them on one, two or all three exercises. Encourage them to listen carefully to the other parent's statements, requests and proposals (while practicing their own skills). Make this a successful experience for both parents, regardless of how much or how little ground you cover in the workbook. Feel free to propose additional meetings about using these four skills to assist them in preparing for communicating, making decisions and supporting each other as parents.

STEP 3: NEW WAYS CHILD SPECIALIST MEETINGS

The parties should already have selected a Child Specialist for their case, who will follow the New Ways process for three meetings with the parents and children. These meetings should occur as soon as possible after the parents have finished their New Ways coaching sessions. The parents shall share the same Child Specialist, who will meet separately with each parent and child/ren, and then jointly with all of them together.

The focus of these sessions is having the parents teach their children the same skills the parents learned in their own Coaching sessions, hearing the children's concerns, and discussing the new ways they will support each other in the new structure of their family.

The Child Specialist should provide these three meetings, using the <u>Collaborative Parent Workbook</u>, as follows:

Session 1:   Teaching Your Child Skills for Resilience

Each parent meets separately with the child/ren and Child Specialist. The focus is the parent teaching the children the four skills of flexible thinking, managed emotions, moderate behaviors and checking yourself. Each parent should do Session 1 with the children before either parent does Session 2. Generally, these sessions should be done during the same week, or within two weeks, so that they remain balanced and each parent reinforces the work of the other parent.

Session 2:   Hearing Your Child's Concerns

Each parent meets separately with the child/ren and the Child Specialist. This session is designed to focus on parents using their four skills, rather than as a counseling session to discuss parent-child relationship difficulties. The focus should be keeping it light and simple, responding at an age-appropriate level to what the child/ren bring up. Each parent should do Session 2 with the children before either parent does Session 3. They can be done in the same week, or within two weeks.

Session 3:   Joint Session – New Ways of Raising Your Child

The two goals of this session are: 1) To explain the new ways that the parents are going to make decisions, communicate, and spend time with the child/ren in the new way the family is organized; and 2) To discuss having the child/ren try some new, moderate behaviors with each parent, with the support of the other parent. These can be fun discussions or serious discussions, and should be presented in an age-appropriate manner. If it would be beneficial, the Child Specialist can meet with each parent separately and with the child/ren separately before, during or after this session. If helpful, there can be additional sessions to address the material and questions in the Collaborative Parent Workbook for this joint session.

Which Parent Meets First?

Which parent meets first with the child/ren for Session 1 can be based on schedules and preferences of the parents. If the child currently favors one parent and resists contact with the other parent, or the child has had no contact with one parent for a while, the first parent to meet with the child should be the "favored" parent. This parent can discuss support for the child meeting with the other parent. Then the meeting with the other parent should occur as soon as possible.

Not Counseling

The Child Specialist meetings are not designed to be intensive parent-child counseling sessions or couples counseling sessions. Instead, they are designed to be an opportunity for the parents to teach skills and then practice using these skills with their children in discussing minor issues of using moderate new behaviors with their children. The focus is laying the groundwork for making decisions in the collaborative process, which is Step 4.

If the parents and/or children need counseling, then appropriate referrals should be made to work with an outside counselor during or after the collaborative divorce process. In general, it is encouraged that both parents participate in any outside parent-child counseling, so that the problems of an imbalance can be jointly addressed, such as when there is a "favored" parent and a "rejected" parent. In general, individual child counseling is to be avoided for the reasons described in the research chapter of this Guidebook. Outside therapists who have been trained in the *New Ways for Families* method would be preferred for referrals, as they are familiar with this method and are usually therapists who are very familiar with high-conflict divorce cases, which have many special dynamics which need to be understood and managed.

STEP 4: FAMILY DECISION-MAKING

Finally, parents use their New Ways skills to develop a lasting parenting plan and to make all other decisions with the assistance of their collaborative team. This step is not structured by the <u>Collaborative Parent Workbook</u>. Once the parents have completed *New Ways for Families* Steps 1, 2 and 3, they should be ready to make decisions within the normal collaborative framework of individual and group meetings with professional team members.

However, a key aspect of Step 4 is that ALL professionals should repeatedly reinforce the use of the three key skills of flexible thinking, managed emotions, and moderate behaviors throughout the decision-making process. For example, all professionals should from time to time ask the following types of questions:

> "Did you have time to "check yourself" for flexible thinking, managed emotions, and moderate behaviors before communicating that idea?"

> "How are you using the 3 skills in making your proposals?"

> "How are you using the 3 skills in communicating with the other party?"

"How are you using the 3 skills in making decisions with the other party?"

"You might want to revise that proposal a little. Do you think the other party might take it as an all-or-nothing approach?"

"Can you think of more than one proposal for this issue?"

"Can you think of how you might prepare yourself to manage your emotions during this meeting? How can I be helpful with that?"

"The other party might view that as an extreme behavior. Can you think of more moderate behaviors you might use in dealing with this problem?"

Reinforcing the 4 Skills

New Ways only begins to train people for using these four conflict-reducing skills. They take practice, especially under stress – and separation and divorce are highly stressful. Yet, divorcing parties can and do use these skills, so that having all collaborative team members regularly reinforce these skills can make a big difference.

Asking parties to "check themselves" for using these skills before making big decisions can help them increase their self-awareness at a time when they can easily become focused on blaming the other party.

They will not be perfect at using these skills. Even after all six sessions of New Ways, they will still make mistakes. They may have an angry outburst or become extremely rigid in their thinking from time to time. It is very important not to criticize them or act as though they have failed at something. Instead, simply ask how they can use the skills now in addressing this decision or problem. The focus is always on the future.

Conclusion

New Ways for Families in Collaborative Divorce is a new method and still in the process of developing, just as the Collaborative Divorce process is still evolving. Yet they are highly compatible methods. It is the author's hope that adding the New Ways method early in the collaborative process will make collaborative process more effective in managing high-conflict families out of court.

Please feel free to contact us for more information, new developments, and to give us your feedback as we develop this method further.

You are encouraged to read the rest of the chapters of this Professional Guidebook, especially if you are facing the types of high-conflict issues described. As Collaborative Divorce grows in usage, there will be more cases with domestic violence, child abuse, child alienation and other such issues. While common wisdom says that these issues are more appropriately handled in court, most experienced family law professionals know that the adversarial structure of court often makes these families worse. In contrast to today's family courts, a collaborative approach has a much better chance of reaching these families and teaching them new skills, with many professionals acting as role-models of flexible thinking, managed emotions, moderate behaviors and checking yourself.

Agreement to Use

New Ways for Families in Collaborative Divorce

We, the undersigned, hereby agree to use the *New Ways for Families* method in our Collaborative Divorce. We agree to the following specific terms:

1. To participate in at least three Coaching sessions which are focused on the material and exercises provided in the New Ways for Families Collaborative Parent Workbook.

2. To obtain our workbooks prior to the first Coaching New Ways session, to write all of the exercises in the Collaborative Parent Workbook when instructed, and to discuss them with our Coach(es).

3. To participate in the first two New Ways Coaching sessions individually, and to participate in the third New Ways Coaching session jointly with the other party.

4. To complete the three New Ways Coaching sessions by _____.

5. To participate in at least three Child Specialist meetings which are focused on the material and exercises provided in the New Ways for Families Collaborative Parent Workbook.

6. To participate in the first two Child Specialist New Ways meetings individually with our child/ren, and to participate in the third Child Specialist New Ways meeting with our children and each other, unless agreed otherwise with the Child Specialist.

7. To complete the three Child Specialist New Ways meetings by _____.

8. That the New Ways for Families Coaching sessions and Child Specialist meetings will be non-confidential, so that our Coach(es) and Child Specialist can discuss any issues addressed in those session with other team members, to the extent they feel it would be beneficial.

9. To make our best efforts to use flexible thinking, managed emotions, and moderate behaviors in our communication with each other, in making our decisions and in parenting our children.

Signature: _____   Signature:_____

Name:_____   Name:_____

Date:_____   Date:_____

Chapter 9

CHAPTER 10
Parenting Coordination and New Ways

New Ways for Families **is highly compatible** with Parenting Coordination. These two methods have the same goals of containing high-conflict families and assisting them in parenting their children despite their frequent conflicts and poor parenting skills. Ideally, potentially high-conflict families would be ordered into (or agree to use) New Ways at the start of their cases; then use Collaborative Divorce, mediation or lawyer settlements to make the decisions in their cases (reinforcing the use of their New Ways skills); and then agree to use a Parenting Coordinator for all future conflicts (reinforcing the use of their New Ways skills). This concept could potentially keep 95% of parenting conflicts out of court, where most experienced professionals believe they do not belong.

Parenting Coordination

Many parents and professionals are not familiar with Parenting Coordination. In short, a Parenting Coordinator generally is appointed by the agreement of the parents and serves to help them make post-divorce decisions about parenting. Usually these are the minor decisions of implementing a parenting court order, rather than the big decisions of who has custody and the basic parenting schedule.

Parenting Coordinators often help parents deal with requests such as switching weekends, arranging pick up times that were not addressed in their court orders, holiday disputes, etc. If the parents cannot reach an agreement, then the Parenting Coordinator decides the issue, in lieu of a judge having to decide the issue at court. This saves a lot of parent time, court time, and lawyer time (if lawyers are involved).

In many states, if a Parenting Coordinator decides the issue, the parents have a certain amount of time (such as ten days) to contest the decision, then it becomes the order of the court if it is not contested. In a sense, the Parenting Coordinator is making a recommendation rather than a decision, but the parents usually do not make the effort to contest the recommendation in court and the judge often orders it anyway. Therefore, Parenting Coordinators are becoming more and more common as a way to save everyone time and money.

Agreeing to Parenting Coordination

However, in most states, the court cannot order parents to have a Parenting Coordinator. They can only stipulate to it by agreement. With potentially high-conflict parents, it is unlikely that they will volunteer for such an approach without experiencing the benefits of out-of-court counseling, coaching and/or settlement. On the other hand, courts in most states can order counseling or parenting classes, which can include *New Ways for Families*.

Once parents are involved in New Ways (by court order or agreement), the New Ways counselors or coaches have several sessions during which they can encourage the use of a Parenting Coordinator ("PC") in the future. This may relieve parents who are concerned that the other parent can take him or her back to court at any time. When there is a PC in the case, they have to return to the PC before they can go to court on a parenting issue.

Parenting Coordinators Recommending New Ways

Parenting Coordinators can recommend New Ways in high-conflict families at any time in the process. In most cases with PCs, they have been appointed (by agreement) after most of the big decisions have been made by the court. These are generally cases that will continue to be high conflict. New Ways can be a useful method for reducing on-going conflicts by expecting the parents to learn the four New Ways skills and practice them in making future decisions.

However, when a Parenting Coordinator recommends New Ways and the court orders it, the PC must make sure to reinforce the parents' use of the New Ways skills. This means that the PC must ask the parents the following questions each time before they discuss any problems or decisions:

"What have you learned in your New Ways sessions?"
"How could you use your skills to address today's problem or decision?"

In other words, the Parenting Coordinator needs to keep the burden on the parents to reinforce the use of their skills. While it is tempting for Parenting Coordinators to focus on making good decisions for the parents, the best situation is for the Parenting Coordinator to reinforce the parents making good decisions by requiring them to demonstrate the use of their skills each time a problem or decision arises.

Following the New Ways Steps

Ideally, if a Parenting Coordinator is involved in a case, he or she should deal with the parents in a similar manner to that of a judge in Step 4: Family (or Court) Decision-Making (see Chapter 6 above). The P.C. should meet with the parents as soon as possible after they finish Step 3 (Parent-Child Counseling), and ask them:

> What have you learned in your New Ways sessions?

> How would you handle a hypothetical parenting situation such as this...? [then ask each of them what they would do in a situation similar to one they had trouble with in the past]

> What situation needs to be addressed today and how could you use your New Ways skills in doing so?

Without having such a meeting immediately after the parents finish with Step 3, the parents are likely to "relapse" and not use their skills with the PC. Parents may assume that the counseling and the legal decision-making are unrelated. Therefore, the PC will make his or her life much easier in the future, if he or she immediately sets the precedent of keeping the burden on the parents to use their New Ways skills.

Example

Suppose a parent sends a reasonable email request to the other parent and the other parent responds with a blaming, attacking, "unmanaged emotions" type of email about the "issue." It will be tempting for a PC to be irritated and focus on the issue. However, it will make the PC's job easier to question the parents and ask: "How can you use your New Ways skills to address this problem? Let's start with revising this email response. How could you do it to show flexible thinking, managed emotions, and moderate behaviors?"

It may be helpful to send the parents back to their Parent-Child Counselor or Collaborative Child Specialist, to practice how they communicate about parenting problems using B.I.F.F. emails and making proposals (see articles "Responding to Hostile Mail (B.I.F.F.)" and "Yes, No, or I'll Think About It" in the Parent Workbook).

Conclusion

New Ways counselors can help promote the benefits of using Parenting Coordinators. Parenting Coordinators can use the New Ways method to help calm and contain high-conflict cases. High-conflict families can be significantly benefited by using New Ways at the front end of potentially high-conflict cases, using out-of-court settlement methods for decision-making (such as Collaborative Divorce, mediation and lawyers settlements), and using PCs at the back end (or as early as possible) of family law cases. Together, these methods can provide a complete alternative to family court for those who can least benefit from it – and who consume the most court resources in self-defeating efforts to "win" issues that really are high-conflict personality issues they can't see.

CHAPTER 11
Research Basis

The development of New Ways for Families is based on a wide range of ideas and research from different sources which can be used to help families. Here is some of the key research which influenced the development of this method.

Parent-Child Interaction Therapy

Parent-Child Interaction Therapy (PCIT) is a method of treating child abuse for parents of children ages 2 – 7 years old. Much of this work is done with parents whose children have been removed from their homes by child protective services workers because of maltreatment. In a relatively short period of time (typically 14-20 sessions), these parents are able to regain custody of their children in their own homes.

In this therapy, the therapist guides the parent and child together in their interactions, teaching and reinforcing positive behaviors. This is done primarily with the therapist behind a two-way mirror in an observation room, who speaks into a microphone which communicates with a blue tooth "bug-in-the-ear" receiver worn by the parent while the parent interacts with the child in a playroom. The theory behind this approach is that working with parents alone or children alone will not stop an abusive cycle. Instead, it is necessary to work on the parent-child interaction, coaching them together to focus on positive behaviors and reduce negative behaviors.

PCIT uses a family systems approach and has had substantial success over the past 15 years, as supported by numerous studies. It was developed at the University of California Davis Children's Hospital, Davis, California. Over 50 mental health treatment agencies provide this method nationwide and internationally. For more information go to **www. pcit.tv.**

New Ways Parent-Child Counseling (Step 2 of *New Ways for Families*) is based on a similar concept of focusing on parent-child interaction, rather than the prevailing Family

Court method with high-conflict divorce families – namely giving the child a separate child therapist and giving one or both parents their own individual therapists. It is necessary to address this interaction, otherwise an abusive parent-child relationship will be strongly resistant to change. While the New Ways Parent-Child Counseling is shorter (only 3 sessions with each parent) and geared to children of all ages, it is believed that the 6 weeks of prior Individual Parent Counseling will help it be successful, as most high-conflict parents have not had their children removed from their care by child protective services.

Child-Inclusive Mediation

Child-Inclusive Mediation includes input from children to their separated parents during the mediation of their parenting disputes. A trained child specialist interviews the children one time, then discusses the children's input with the parents and their mediator one time. This child-inclusive divorce mediation approach has been found to be significantly more effective than comparable mediation which only includes generic child-focused developmental information provided by the mediator.

Research comparing the child-inclusive method and the child-focused generic method indicates that the child-inclusive parenting agreements were longer-lasting and the parents were half as likely to return to court to litigate parenting matters a year later. Apparently the child-inclusive parents were more emotionally available to their children after learning of their concerns, more able to work together for the benefit of their children, and provided more stable care throughout the year.

This research was done in Australia by Jennifer McIntosh, Ph.D., and others with the Family Transitions clinic based in Melbourne. For more information about this method see:

McIntosh, J. E., Wells, Y. D., Smyth, B. M., & Long, C. M. (2008). Child-Focused and Child-Inclusive Divorce Mediation: Comparative Outcomes from a Prospective Study of Postseparation Adjustment. Family Court Review, 46, 105-124.

New Ways Parent-Child Counseling is intended to incorporate this approach more directly by having each parent and child meet together three times, with the assistance of the Parent-Child Counselor. The first session focuses on the parent teaching the child skills, while the second session focuses on the parent listening to the child's concerns. Based on the impact of this second session, after hearing directly of their children's concerns, most parents are expected to be more able to negotiate a realistic parenting plan and will be less interested in fighting in court over their children.

Dialectical Behavior Therapy

Dialectical Behavior Therapy was developed to specifically address the problems of people with Borderline Personality Disorder. Traditionally, personality disorders have been considered non-treatable. However, extensive research over the past 15 years has shown success by several approaches to treating Borderline Personality Disorder, with Dialectical Behavior Therapy (DBT) demonstrating some of the greatest success.

This therapy includes an individual therapist, a skills building group therapy, and a consultation group for the therapists. The key elements are teaching small skills in small steps and lots of validation of the person along the way. The individual therapist deals with the many emotions and set-backs which occur for those with this disorder. Obvious lessons require much repetition and support by a therapist who does not become overwhelmed or blaming.

People with Borderline Personality Disorder are particularly identified by their unconscious defense mechanism of "splitting" – a belief that those around them are either all-good or all-bad. Because of this symptom, those who work with this population must be constantly vigilant to avoid "professional splitting" – absorbing the intense distress of the BPD client and becoming angry and blaming of each other as professionals. Therefore, DBT's success is dependent on all professionals working together to remain positive and focused on small steps of progress.

Emotion "dysregulation" is also a characteristic of those with Borderline Personality Disorder. Learning to manage one's own emotions is a focus of DBT. For professionals, avoiding getting emotionally hooked by these heightened and unmanaged emotions is one of the most important aspects of this work. It often takes substantial training.

This method was developed by Marsha Linehan, Ph.D., at the University of Washington in Seattle, Washington. For more information about DBT: www.BehavioralTech. org. For a recent book on applying this approach to different settings see: Dimeff, L. A. & Koerner, K. (2007). Dialectical Behavior Therapy in Clinical Practice: Applications Across Disorders and Settings. New York, NY: Guilford Publications, Inc.

New Ways Individual Parent Counseling is based on similar concepts: Teaching small skills in small steps, the need for an individual therapist to help the client deal with constant resistance to change, and that all professionals need to work together to support the client's efforts to learn skills. Traditionally, Family Court professionals are known for showing strong disdain and criticism toward the "opposing" parent in court, heatedly arguing over who is to blame, and either expecting dramatic change immediately based on a lecture or expecting no change ever. New Ways Individual Counseling gives parents a chance to change before decisions are made.

High-Conflict Personalities

Recent research indicates that personality disorders have become a significant percentage of the general population. They have characteristics that are common to high-conflict family court disputes, so that understanding the dynamics and treatment of these disorders is helpful to handling high-conflict court cases.

The National Epidemiologic Survey on Alcohol and Related Conditions funded by the National Institutes of Health studied personality disorders (among other mental disorders) based on a sample of 43,093 people in 2001-2002 and 2004-2005 in the United States. The overall rate of personality disorders in the general population was determined to be approximately 20%.

Personality disorders were associated with significant interpersonal dysfunction and feelings of distress in this study. More specifically, the personality disorders often associated with legal disputes (the "Cluster B" personality disorders) were much higher than in the previous research provided by the Diagnostic and Statistical Manual of Mental Disorders of the American Psychiatric Association, currently known as the DSM-IV, which was based on research from before 1994 when it first was published. The DSM-IV-TR ("Text Revision") was published in 2000, but it did not provide any new data on personality disorder prevalence.

The NIH study results for the Cluster B personality disorders are as follows:

Borderline Personality Disorder	=	5.9% of general population
Narcissistic Personality Disorder	=	6.2% of general population
Antisocial Personality Disorder	=	3.6% of general population
Histrionic Personality Disorder	=	1.8% of general population

There is a significant overlap among these disorders, so that nearly 40% of those with one of these personality disorders has another. Therefore, approximately 8-10% of the general population may have a Cluster B personality disorder.

The significance of Cluster B personality disorders is that they tend to be high drama, high energy and high conflict. They also tend to run much higher in families where another relative has a personality disorder. For example, the DSM-IV-TR indicates that Borderline Personality Disorder is about five times more likely to occur in families with another first-degree relative with the disorder than in the general population.

For more information see:

American Psychiatric Association. (2000). Diagnostic and statistical manual of mental disorders (4th ed., text revised). Washington, DC.

Grant, B. F., Hasin, D. S., Stinson, R. S., Dawson, D. A., Chou, S. P., Ruan, W. J. et al (2004). Prevalence, correlates, and disability of personality disorders in the United States: Results from the National Epidemiologic Survey on Alchol and Related Conditions. Journal of Clinical Psychiatry, 65, 948-958.

Grant, B. F., Chou, S. P., Goldstein, R. B., Huang, B., Stinson, F. S., Saha, T. D., et al (2008). Prevalence, correlates, disability and comorbidity of DSM-IV Borderline Personality disorder: Results from the Wave 2 national epidemiologic survey on alcohol and related conditions. Journal of Clinical Psychiatry, 69, 533-545.

Stinson, R. S., Dawson, D. A., Goldstein, R. B. Chou, S. P., Huang, B., Smith, S. M. et al (2008). Prevalence, correlates, disability, and comorbity of DSM-IV Narcissistic Personality Disorder: Results from the Wave 2 National Epidemiologic Survey on Alchol and Related Conditions. Journal of Clinical Psychiatry, 69, 1033-1045.

New Ways Individual Parent Counseling is based on the possibility that many high-conflict parents have personality disorders or traits. In that case, it is especially important to have individual counseling to form a secure relationship with them to help them learn to manage all-or-nothing thinking, unmanaged emotions, and extreme behavior. A parenting class alone may be insufficient to accomplish this difficult task, although parenting classes following this method may be very helpful.

There are many other methods and ideas that have influenced the development of New Ways, but the most influential are described above. The main point is that potentially high-conflict parents need a lot of structure, small steps for learning, and lots of validation. These are all essential to the *New Ways for Families* method.

CHAPTER 12
Adaptation for Specific Cases and Budgets

The basic 4-Step structure of this process can be adapted by agreement of the parents or by the courts, while retaining its basic structure and goals. Common adaptations could include the following, after Step 1: Getting Started.

Step 2

Additional Individual Sessions: Since the individual counseling is confidential, the counseling relationship should remain intact after the 6 sessions are over and even after parenting decisions have been made. At the request of the parent, there could be occasional sessions in the future. The court could also order additional sessions, such as another 6 weeks, if it appears it would be beneficial.

As part of a Parenting Class: See Chapter Eight.

Earlier Review Hearing: If a court orders temporary supervised visitation or no contact for one of the parents when ordering *New Ways for Families*, the court may choose to have a Review Hearing immediately following Step 1 in 6 weeks, rather than waiting the full 12 weeks after both Step 1 and Step 2 have been completed. This way these restrictions are less likely to develop a life of their own and may be reduced after only 6 weeks if sufficient progress is demonstrated.

In Collaborative Divorce: See Chapter Nine.

Court Mediators: If a court system has mediators addressing parenting conflicts, a mediator could recommend *New Ways for Families* (Steps 2 and 3), then meet with the parents afterward (generally 12 weeks later) to mediate their final parenting plan, before going before the judge. This may possibly make a court hearing unnecessary at both ends of the process. Ideally, the court would order New Ways and schedule a mediation session at the end of the 12 weeks, so that the mediator only needs to meet with the parents once, when they are most ready to be realistic and productive.

Private Mediation: In cases of parenting disputes or concerns, a private divorce mediator could encourage or recommend that the parents participate in *New Ways for Families* either concurrently with mediation sessions or after the first session and before returning for future sessions. Participating in New Ways prior to mediation should allow for a more productive mediation process.

Settlement with Lawyers: In cases with lawyers, they could schedule joint settlement meetings after Step 2 with their clients to begin developing a long-term parenting schedule and possibly other agreements such as financial issues. If they can reach an agreement, then they will not need to prepare for litigation of past behavior when they get to Step 4 in court, or court hearings will no longer be necessary. Step 3 (Parent-Child Counseling) is still encouraged, even if they reach an agreement after Step 2, so that the parents can teach their children skills for resilience and to keep the family from becoming high conflict later on.

Step 3

Combined Parent Session: The third session for each parent with the child/ren could be a combined meeting with both parents meeting with the child/ren, with the assistance of the Parent-Child Counselor. If it appears that both parents are ready to work together at this level, this could be a significant benefit for the children and help the parents work together in the future.

Future Parent-Child Sessions: The parents could always request assistance from the Parent-Child Counselor in the future. Of course, this should be a joint decision and not made by only one parent and the counselor. Otherwise, the counselor may be pulled into the adversarial process, which New Ways is structured to avoid.

Confidential vs. Non-Confidential: In less adversarial cases, the Parent-Child Counseling could be confidential, just as the individual parent counseling is confidential. However, in cases that are likely to require the court to make parenting decisions, it would be helpful to be non-confidential, so that the court can ask specific questions of the Parent-Child Counselor. This could include each parent's level of appropriateness in discussing issues with the child/ren, cooperation with the counseling process, and demonstrated ability of each parent to reflect on past behavior and change negative behavior. Ideally, the Parent-Child Counselor would not write a report about the counseling for the court, as it would pull the counselor into the adversarial contest and impair this counselor's ability to provide future assistance to the family.

In Collaborative Divorce: See Chapter Nine.

Step 4

<u>Parenting Coordinator</u>: See Chapter Ten.

<u>Assessing for Domestic Violence</u>: With the advent of the Wingspread Conference has come a new emphasis on distinguishing among several forms of domestic violence. The nature of and success of each parent's behavior in Steps 2 and 3 could provide a partial assessment to indicate which category a parent's potential fits into regarding the need for treatment (batterer's treatment group, anger management, conflict resolution training, more individual counseling or other).

<u>Review Hearing</u>: Depending on the case, the court could schedule a Review Hearing in 3, 6, 12 or more months, to help contain the case and to help motivate parents to complete future tasks. However, ideally no further court hearings would need to be scheduled if the parents have demonstrated an increased ability to handle matters on their own or with the help of a Parenting Coordinator.

CHAPTER 13
Handling Abuse and Alienation in New Ways

High-conflict cases in Family Court usually include allegations of child abuse, domestic violence, child alienation, substance abuse or false allegations. The usual course of events is that the court immediately makes restricted parenting orders based on these allegations. Often this is how a high-conflict case starts, with restrictive parenting orders made at the very first emergency hearing, where only one party is present making this request.

Ultimately, the court may maintain these restrictions (supervised visitation, etc.) over the long term, or set them aside after hearing more information as the case progresses. However, the emphasis is on determining the seriousness of the perpetrator's past behavior and then making commensurate court orders.

New Ways for Families takes a different approach. While temporary restrictive orders may be necessary, the emphasis is not on determining the seriousness of the perpetrator's prior behavior alone, but also the ability of that parent to change his or her behavior. Behavior change is the focus, rather than past behavior alone. Past behavior is often a predictor of future behavior, but for many parents their behavior is based on isolated incidents or behavior patterns which could be changed with a structured counseling program including small steps, lots of validation, and a well-trained therapist for this specific purpose.

Ideally, when a parent expresses concern that the other parent may have some parenting problems, the initial focus should be on treatment rather than simply on long-term restrictive parenting. While restrictive parenting may be necessary, treatment over time may make a balanced parenting plan more appropriate. The goal should be parent training, not parent exclusion. This will reduce the high-conflict nature of many family court cases and protect children from developing their own extreme personalities.

Child Abuse

There are many forms of child abuse, with child neglect being the most common. As described in the research chapter of this Guidebook, there has been much success in treating child abuse. Counselors using the *New Ways for Families* method should be adequately informed of treatment programs and methods for addressing child abuse in separated and divorced families. By misunderstanding these issues, counselors can escalate a case into high conflict unnecessarily. Change, not exclusion, should be the goal.

Child Alienation

This highly controversial subject is too large to address sufficiently here. The subject of child alienation has been often referred to as Parental Alienation Syndrome. However, most mental health professionals and legal professionals have not adopted the term as a "syndrome." The causes of children's resistance to spending time with one parent are too many to be identified as one specific syndrome. The more commonly used term by professionals in the court system is "child alienation," as defined by Joan Kelly, Ph.D. and Janet Johnston, Ph. D. They consider a variety of reasons for a child's refusal, including normal developmental preferences, alignments specific to the divorce, and estrangement from a neglectful or abusive parent.

For more information see:

Kelly, J. & Johnston, J. (2001). The Alienated Child: A reformulation of parental alienation syndrome. Family Court Review, 39, 249-266.

Johnston, J., Roseby, V., & Kuehnle, K. (2009). In the Name of the Child: A Developmental Approach to Understanding and Helping Children of Conflicted and Violent Divorce. Springer.

After handling many alienation cases, this author believes that both parents often contribute in many ways, primarily unconsciously, to the child's alienation in high-conflict separations and divorces. The four skills which are the focus of this Guidebook are the same four skills that parents need to develop to prevent child alienation. In most alienation cases, there has been a pattern of all-or-nothing thinking, unmanaged emotions, and extreme behaviors demonstrated by both parents – "justified" by the other parent's behavior. In subtle little ways, both parents may contribute to these characteristics inadvertently, some more than others.

While it is true that some parents engage in knowingly alienating behaviors with their children, this author believes that the larger problem is the unconscious patterns described above, which have often been in place for years before the separation.

For example, it is common for a favored parent to emphasize to the child that the rejected parent is a negative person and to withhold all positive comments regarding the rejected parent. While some negative characteristics may exist (as they do with all human beings), the lack of recognition of any positive qualities reinforces all-or-nothing thinking – which may be absorbed by the child totally unconsciously. While the parent has been "truthful" in expressing some specific criticisms of the rejected parent, the parent has not been realistic by excluding a larger, more flexible view of the other parent. This negative focus may have started with the separation, or may have been a pattern throughout the child's life.

For another example, in some cases a rejected parent asks the child if he or she really wants the rejected parent to stop having any contact. If the alienation has become significant, the child says "yes," and the rejected parent withdraws from the child's life – thereby reinforcing that all-or-nothing solutions and extreme behavior are appropriate in solving relationship problems. While this is understandable behavior by a rejected parent, it reinforces the characteristics that have been in place – sometimes for many years even before the separation.

While the traditional approach has been to fight over which parent is to blame for abusing or purposely alienating the child, this approach has universally failed to solve problems while escalating parents into a high-conflict court case. Therefore, it is very important for all professionals working with potentially high-conflict parents to take a prevention approach that emphasizes flexible thinking, managed emotions, moderate behaviors and checking yourself.

Using the Steps of New Ways to Reduce Risk

STEP 1: GETTING STARTED

New Ways can be ordered by the judge at a hearing, or agreed to by signed stipulation of the parties. The order or stipulation does not assign blame to either parent, and puts both parents into the identical counseling structure.

Prior to beginning the counseling step of New Ways, each parent is expected to prepare a "Behavioral Declaration" which focuses on specific problem behavior of the other parent, in a very limited space, namely two pages. By so limiting this declaration, it does not reinforce the escalation of highly emotional and all-or-nothing allegations against the other parent. It discourages the attack on the other parent as a whole person, with no redeeming qualities. It focuses on "problem behaviors" rather than the person.

This declaration also includes three statements by each parent describing the positive qualities of the other parent. This goes against their automatic rigid, all-or-nothing thinking. In alienation cases, it is common for one or both parents to only speak in negative terms and to withhold any positive recognition of behaviors or skills of the other parent.

In addition to the behavioral Declaration, each parent prepares a Reply Behavioral Declaration (in reply to the other parent's concerns expressed in his or her Behavioral Declaration). This Reply Behavior Declaration allows the parent the opportunity to acknowledge behavior problems and to say how he or she intends to work on those problems. This reduces the pressure to simply defend one's own past behavior. Instead, it focuses on developing positive new behaviors.

If all professionals involved in a case encourage the acknowledgment of problems and help the parents focus on making efforts for positive future behavior, it is expected that less pressure will pass to the children to take sides in the parents' dispute.

If attorneys are encouraged to explain and support this emphasis on positive future behavior with their clients, it is expected that there will be less anxiety for the clients and more ability to consider new ways of parenting in the future.

Lastly, in some jurisdictions, the parents each pick their own Individual Parent Counselor from a list of therapists trained in *New Ways for Families*. This shows respect for the parents and reinforces their role in decision-making regarding the separation or divorce, which may reduce their anxiety and fears of losing of control.

STEP 2: INDIVIDUAL PARENT COUNSELING

The focus of the Individual Parent Counseling is practicing the four basic skills (flexible thinking, managed emotions, moderate behaviors, and checking yourself), rather than on blaming the other parent.

The New Ways Parent Workbook repeatedly encourages the parent to write down and think about these skills. This is an encouraging process, without blame, criticism or shame. The focus is repeatedly on future behavior. The therapist and the client discuss current problem situations and how to address them using these new skills ("new ways").

Whenever the parent blames the other parent in the discussions, the counselor can say "how could you use flexible thinking to address this situation?" Or: "How could you use managed emotions to help solve this problem?" Or : "What moderate behaviors could you use in response to the other parent or your child to manage this problem?" When a parent starts blaming the other parent or is concerned the other parent is getting away with things, his or her counselor can say: "Remember, the other parent is working on the same issues in the same workbook." This way each parent can be directed back to their own behavior, knowing that the other parent is being told the same thing.

In some cases, one parent may be "high conflict" and the other may already be reasonable as a parent and may already use these skills regularly. In this case, the counselor for the reasonable parent can reinforce these skills as ways to help deal with and in some cases "manage" the more difficult parent. By responding with moderate behaviors to the difficult parent's extreme behaviors, a reasonable parent may be able to calm the dispute.

The way this parallel counseling is structured, a counselor doesn't have to decide which parent is more difficult, but can reinforce using these skills to manage the other parent regardless of whether he or she is really the more difficult parent.

This method creates a non-defensive, non-blaming environment, which is absolutely necessary for new skills to be practiced and truly learned. The usual high-conflict environment of cases with allegations of child abuse and/or parental alienation, actually prevents behavior change from occurring and new skills from being learned. New Ways is structured in the opposite direction so that learning new skills can take place.

In some cases, one or both parents will be unable to learn and demonstrate these low conflict skills of flexible thinking, managed emotions and moderate behaviors. In these cases, they will be unable to reach agreements and make their own parenting decisions. They will end up back in court and the judge can observe their learning (or not) regarding these skills.

A parent cannot get a Verification of Completion signed by his or her therapist, until he or she has completed six full individual counseling sessions and completed his or her Parent Workbook, as well as the Behavioral Declaration and Reply Declarations. This gives a motivation to the parent to complete the process and to work within the New Ways structure, rather than missing appointments or being preoccupied with blaming the other parent in traditionally less-structured counseling sessions.

STEP 3: PARENT-CHILD COUNSELING

The Parent-Child Counselor is specifically assigned by the court or jointly selected by the parents (and their attorneys, if any). In either case, the Parent-Child Counselor starts in a neutral position and is appointed as a neutral expert for the court. This counselor will only be provided each party's Behavioral Declaration, Reply Behavioral Declaration and related court orders. This helps the Parent-Child Counselor avoid being pulled into an adversarial decision-making role for the parents. It prevents them from swamping the counselor with highly emotional declarations which detail every "transgression" of the other parent. It also helps keep the focus on future behavior rather than past negative behavior.

However, the Parent-Child Counselor will be aware of the worst allegations against each parent from their brief statements in their Behavioral Declarations. The Parent-Child Counselor can address these issues in a productive way, rather than becoming emotionally hooked with the volume of allegations and detail that usually arrives in their office in documents.

The Parent-Child counseling is structured to keep parents on an equal basis, in terms of number of appointments involving the child and the order of issues addressed.

The first of three sessions for each parent focuses on having the parent teach the children the four low conflict skills of flexible thinking, managed emotions, moderate behaviors and checking yourself. By having each parent teach these same skills to the children, the children learn that both parents support these skills. In addition, the children learn that the parents are expected to be using these skills. In other words, the child is discouraged from forming a negative alliance with a parent around all-or-nothing thinking, unmanaged emotions, and extreme behaviors. The child will know that these are "officially" incorrect behaviors. This will help the child resist a "good parent" and a "bad parent" view of their family. In reality, alienated or estranged children are primarily demonstrating those three negative behaviors in concert with one or both parents.

The second session for each parent (which cannot occur until both parents have completed the first parent-child session), focuses on each parent hearing the children's concerns about the separation or divorce. This also helps deal with the alienation issue, because the child sees that each parent is open to the child's feedback, with the assistance of the Parent-Child Counselor. In other words, the child can complain to their parents, which is a helpful thing as part of growing up. In the process, the Parent-Child Counselor helps direct the parent to receive the child's concerns without judgment, without anger and without giving in.

When the child experiences an "all-bad parent" actually listening in a non-judgmental manner, it may loosen up their all-or-nothing view of that parent. Also, when the child experiences the "all-good parent" actually listening to the child's negative concerns, the child will be encouraged to take a more flexible approach, rather than having to absolutely treat that parent as "all good." This experience should assist the child in being less alienated or estranged. This may take a lot of repetition in many more-severe cases.

The third session of Parent-Child counseling focuses on how each parent and child may act in new ways towards each other and toward the other parent. This should create a momentum towards change in the relationship of the child with each parent. By the "all-good parent" encouraging the child to move forward with activities with the "all-bad parent," the child will learn that he or she has permission to have a more reasonable and balanced relationship with each parent. By meeting with the "all-bad parent," the child will learn that steps are going to occur to re-engage the child with that parent. The steps may need to be small, but inevitable.

Positive reinforcement and negative reinforcement for re-engagement with the "all-bad parent" will nudge the child forward. This is much more desirable than the all-or-nothing thinking that is applied to many alienation cases, in which a child is simply moved from one parent to the other, in a very dramatic and controversial manner. While the author will not rule out that this may be appropriate in a very small number of extreme cases, it should only be used when the New Ways method has been thoroughly tried first. The author's belief is that by using this approach earlier in potentially high-conflict cases, that the number of cases that would reach such an extreme intervention will be very, very small - much smaller than exists today.

On the other hand, there may be some cases in which there is domestic violence or child abuse, and it is appropriate that the child is primarily with the "all-good parent." However, even in these cases, it is very important for the child to learn that no parent is truly "all-good" and that no parent is not truly "all-bad." Such an all-or-nothing approach to both parents is harmful to the child's upbringing, sense of self, and sense of others in close relationships. It interferes with learning which behaviors are appropriate for healthy relationships. If a child learns that everything that one parent does is good, than the child does not learn to distinguish that parent's healthy behaviors and unhealthy behaviors. If a child learns that one parent is all bad and that everything he or she does is all-bad, then the child does not learn to distinguish that parent's healthy behaviors and unhealthy behaviors.

No Contact Between Parents

The parent-child counseling, as well as the individual parent counseling, is designed so that neither parent needs to have contact with the other parent during the entire process. This helps prevent high-conflict encounters, and protects a victim parent from an abusive parent. Therefore, this method can be safely used with parents in which there are allegations of domestic violence and or child abuse, as well as alienation or estrangement. These issues don't have to be resolved in order to enter and learn skills in *New Ways for Families*. By avoiding judgments of blame and a preoccupation with past behavior, while also protecting children and parents, the family has a chance to learn new behaviors that will be more helpful in the long run than any judgments regarding past behavior.

Temporary court orders before the counseling begins, and future court orders after it is over, can still provide protection for a parent and/or children, and future findings can still be made. However, the focus is to be on future behavior. There are so many high-conflict families with children that we cannot just accept their failure. For the sake of their children, we need to teach their parents skills for successfully raising their children – so that they do not also become high-conflict parents! New Ways has duel goals: Protection against abuse and/or alienation, while focusing on teaching positive skills.

Lastly, the Parent-Child counselor observes the parent behavior with the children in these three sessions each. By observing three sessions with each parent, the counselor can see an ability to change after receiving feedback and direction from the counselor. Ideally the parents will settle their parenting issues immediately after the parent-child counseling, possibly even before the third session. However, in cases where settlement cannot occur, because of one or both parents' inability to develop positive skills, then the family will go to court. In that case, the Parent-Child counselor can testify at court at the request of either parent or the judge.

However, this counselor does not write a report, as reports tend to escalate parents into high-conflict behavior and posturing. Instead, if the parties are able to settle their case, there will be no information that goes to the court other than the completion of the Parent-Child Counseling and their settlement agreement. If they are unable to settle, then that counselor can testify about what was observed. Traditionally, evaluations and reports tend to inspire defensive behavior, more than they resolve. New Ways is designed to avoid escalating into high-conflict behavior.

However, since the Parent-Child counselor can testify at court, the court can have current information about each parents' parenting behavior, which is much more useful than reports of what each parent did several months or years ago. In addition, the Parent-Child counselor can report on each parents' ability to change his or her behavior. It's this ability to change which is the focus of new behaviors and helping families move into positive directions rather than negative, all-or-nothing "attack and defend" cycles of behavior, which inherently spill over to their children and inherently develop into child alienation in many cases.

STEP 4: FAMILY (OR COURT) DECISION MAKING

In this last stage of the *New Ways for Families* process, the parents make their own decisions, if possible. All the professionals involved in the case are encouraged to support the parents in making their own decisions, rather than trying to make decisions for them. This may include attorneys, court mediators, private mediators, collaborative professionals, or others. At no time do the parents have to meet together in order to reach a settlement. Even in cases of domestic violence, child abuse, etc, parents can stipulate to future treatment programs (such as drug treatment, batterer's treatment, etc,) and to parenting classes, without having to go to court. The New Ways Individual Counseling and Parent-Child Counseling can be used to encourage settlement and acceptance of the need for future change. It is expected that some parents who have engaged in negative behaviors will agree to accept treatment for those behaviors, rather than having to go to court and have them publicly discussed.

If the parents are unable to reach their own agreements, then they can always go before the judge. Rather than starting out the case with allegations against each other, the judge asks parents to report what each has learned from their counseling in New Ways. This places the burden equally on each parent to explain what he or she has learned, and allows the judge an open-minded opportunity to hear how realistic each parent is. A reasonable parent will be able to talk easily in terms that demonstrate flexible thinking, managing emotions and moderate behaviors. In addition, reasonable parents using this process will feel safe to admit some of their own short comings and things they have learned to do better.

On the other hand, a parent who continues to demonstrate unreasonable behaviors will expose him or herself to the court as unable to admit past short comings and unable to describe new learnings - because he or she does not believe they need to change and learn anything. Such reports will help the court.

After asking for a report of what each parent has learned, then the judge should quiz the parents on problem parenting scenarios based on their Behavioral Declarations. In this process, the court will listen for realistic self-awareness of problems and solutions. The burden is on each parent to explain what he or she has learned, rather than on the report of an expert that was written before the hearing. This also helps reduce the likelihood of alienation and high-conflict behavior. The parent will prepare for this hearing by acting in a more positive manner rather than in a more negative manner. This emphasis on demonstrating one's own positive skills, rather than emphasizing blame of the other, may help reduce the conflict in the family, which may help reduce the pressure on the children to take sides.

Only after reporting back leanings and demonstrating new solutions to old problems, will the parents be able to fight about each other in the court hearing. Only after the court has formed his or her own impression of each parent's abilities, will the court hear testimony and argument for and against each parent.

New Ways for Families is designed in this way to block high-conflict behaviors and to reinforce the use of positive skills. This is a new method and is being tried in several cases. For the reasons described above, attorneys, courts and therapists are encouraged to try this new approach to handling child alienation as well as other high-conflict issues in family court.

CHAPTER 14
Handling Domestic Violence in New Ways

The purpose of this chapter is to address how *New Ways for Families* can be used in domestic violence cases to reduce the conflict between the parents, move both parents closer to getting needed help, provide useful parenting information, and serve as a partial assessment tool for the court in making future orders.

Domestic violence is an area of growing concern in family courts, as highlighted by the 2007 Wingspread Conference and Report sponsored by Association of Family and Conciliation Courts (AFCC) and National Council of Juvenile and Family Court Judges (NCJFCJ). Differentiating among at least four different types of domestic violence is recognized as very important, yet in reality the adversarial court process often clouds these issues more than clarifies them. Various assessment tools are being considered, and New Ways may be used as an additional partial assessment tool.

Historically, family law professionals have not recognized the significance of domestic violence risks in some cases and have exaggerated concerns in others. In the process, some partners and children have been seriously injured or killed, while other children have lost a meaningful relationship with one of their parents because of unnecessarily-restrictive parenting orders. New Ways may offer some assistance in addressing this problem, by providing non-judgmental, parallel counseling before the conflict escalates and before long-term decisions are made, while still making temporary protective orders.

Problems in Domestic Violence Cases in Family Courts

Problems of safety: The top priority is always safety – for the victim and the children. This is often addressed by seeking and obtaining 100-yard temporary restraining orders, residence exclusion orders, and temporary no contact orders or supervised visitation between the perpetrator and the children. Yet victims often receive no counseling and tend to underestimate the risk of injury despite the restraining orders (no paper ever stopped a bullet), including initiating contact with the perpetrator. Victims often change their minds and they do not return to court to obtain a permanent restraining order in many (perhaps a majority) of cases.

Likewise, the perpetrator often gets no counseling at this early point in the legal process and may attempt to stalk the victim or pressure the victim to reconcile. The time of separation is the highest risk for violence, yet there is no structure for focusing the intense emotions each party is feeling. Temporary restrictive parenting orders often get continued as the legal process inches forward, especially when custody evaluations are ordered. Children may go weeks before seeing one parent and, in some cases, may reside solely with a parent who has a mental health problem and/or has made exaggerated or false claims.

Problems differentiating types of domestic violence: Following the Wingspread Conference, four very different types of domestic violence have been analyzed and different legal responses have been determined appropriate for each:

Coercive Controlling Violence ("battering," risk of serious injuries, pattern of control and fear);

Situational Couple Violence (mutual violence, few injuries, no pattern of control and fear);

Separation-Instigated Violence (1-2 incidents at separation, no history of violence); and

Violent Resistance (by a victim to stop the violence, but higher risk of getting injured).

Yet distinguishing among these four types is not easy, as they often look the same on the surface. A slap on the face could have occurred in any of the above types. It could be the warning sign of intense intimidation that reinforces past years of fear and a serious threat for future violence for a victim of Coercive Controlling Violence. If you underestimate this risk, a victim could get seriously hurt or become isolated and severely depressed.

Or it may have been a single occurrence, or both parties may have equally engaged in aggressive behavior. If you overestimate this problem, then orders severely restricting parent contact with children may start a downward spiral of one parent giving up or a child becoming alienated against that restricted parent.

Problems with the adversarial process of assessment: Types and severity of domestic violence are difficult to assess even in the absence of litigation. But in the adversarial process, emotions often run so high that serious abuse is excused or ignored, or that isolated incidents are exaggerated. To be safe, courts often make orders based on the worst case scenario. This can reinforce false or exaggerated claims. On the other hand, after seeing several emotionally-exaggerated cases, some legal professionals have developed a presumption that domestic violence reports are strategic tactics in separation or divorce litigation and therefore all lack merit. Decisions are made at highly emotional hearings, where perpetrators can be very controlled and look good, while victims risk being seen as overly dramatic and lacking credibility. Often attorneys present opposing arguments with great intensity, when they actually have little meaningful information.

In the adversarial process, parents become rigid in their positions and become closed to any change in their own future behavior. Perpetrators feel driven to put all of their energy into defending or denying their prior abusive behavior. The price of being found guilty of domestic violence in family law cases is very high: loss of meaningful contact with children, increased financial obligations (in California spousal support can be affected by a history of domestic violence), and possible loss of liberty (going to jail).

Victims and their advocates are appropriately strong in putting forward the position that they have not "caused" the abuse they have experienced. They need to be strong, because professionals have traditionally blamed them as part of the problem. To suggest that a victim go into counseling could be seen as punishing the victim, and may be seen by the court or the other side as admitting to some responsibility for being abused. However, this is tragic, because victims can benefit so much from counseling to prevent being a victim in the future.

Victims are often in extreme distress and their own denial, and they often return to their greatest source of past reassurance – ironically, the perpetrator. This is a highly-reinforcing cycle of intimacy and anger, especially as the victim feels a loss of self-esteem and fear of criticism from professionals for making bad decisions regardless of what she (or he) does. Many experienced domestic violence professionals understand that victim education is an important part of ending the cycle.

How New Ways Can Address These Problems

New Ways for Families is partially designed to address these problems, as follows:

Step 1: Ordering New Ways

When the court first orders New Ways, temporary orders can be made (TROs, restricted parenting, etc.), at the same time as both parents are ordered into the counseling of New Ways. The judge can keep the conflict from escalating by stating that he or she makes no assumptions about which parent is accurate in describing their dispute and about how serious the abuse is, or if there is abuse at all. All of this will be determined by the court in the last step of New Ways, after the counseling steps. This helps keep both parents from focusing on defending a position, and instead on following the court's orders for the short-term, structured counseling.

Step 2: Individual Parent Counseling

As each party will meet with their own confidential counselor for six sessions (usually over six weeks), this is a safe setting for victims to address the reality of their situation without having to be blamed for the abuse. They can gain strength from their individual counselor, as well as education and strategies for self-protection. Over six weeks, victims may develop the confidence to explain the abuse more clearly to the court, and also may gain more confidence to separate (and stay separated) from their abuser. All of this is without any contact necessary with the perpetrator. In cases of distorted claims of abuse, the counselor can educate the client about the dynamics of abuse, the risks of misleading allegations, and available treatments for the client's possible mental health problems. Long-term decisions are delayed while this counseling is occurring, so that they do not have to meet together in parenting mediation or at court. Yet it is also time-limited, so that the client knows the counseling is not open-ended and that work needs to be done with the time available. However, clients can extend the counseling by request, so that if a good relationship is established with the counselor there can be ongoing support, even if it is in less frequent sessions.

For perpetrators, or alleged perpetrators, the individual counseling is an opportunity for reality-testing and focusing on his (or her) own behavior. The counselor can educate this party on the options and potential consequences of past and future violent behavior. Yet at the same time, the counselor can give the client some hope for changing future behavior, by beginning to learn the four basic skills of New Ways (flexible thinking, managed emotions, moderate behaviors, and checking yourself), and applying them to possible parenting situations. This is not the end in most cases, but the beginning of accepting other treatments for domestic violence, including batterer's treatment (in cases of Coercive Controlling Violence) or anger management (in cases of Situational Couple Violence or Separation-Instigated Violence). Ideally, such clients will be more willing to stipulate to ongoing restraining orders and a batterers treatment program or other future treatment, after discussing it in the supportive setting of confidential counseling, rather than the confrontational public setting of courtroom litigation.

Step 3: Parent-Child Counseling

The third step of *New Ways for Families* is three highly-structured sessions for each parent alone with the child/ren, alternating weeks with the other parent, using the same Parent-Child Counselor. No contact between the parents is necessary, although in some cases they may agree to meet together in the final session to discuss new family arrangements, schedules, communication methods, and decision-making. Such a joint final meeting could productively occur in cases of Situational Couple Violence or Separation-Instigated Violence, but would not be advised for cases of Coercive Controlling Violence.

In many domestic violence cases, the parents are going to have a Parallel Parenting arrangement, such that they do not have direct contact at exchanges (which would be done at school by each parent separately, etc.), they have highly limited communication (such as one email maximum on child-only issues a day), and they have few (if any) decisions to make jointly. In such an arrangement, each parent can have significant time with the children, based on his or her own parenting skills. The Parent-Child Counseling can realistically prepare the parents and children for this new way of parenting.

In the Parent-Child Counseling, the counselor can observe each parent's ability to communicate supportively with their children and observe each parent's openness to changing their communication patterns. The counselor can also observe the child's level of comfort with each parent, and whether a child appears to have been coached or intimidated by either parent. By seeing each parent with the children in alternating weeks, the counselor can observe the contrasts in each parents' overall capability.

Ideally, after Step 2 of New Ways, parents in domestic violence families will be more able to make their own realistic decisions out of court by agreement, with the help of professionals, such as attorneys, court mediators, etc. This would include stipulating to ongoing restraining orders, possible future counseling orders, parenting classes, and Parallel Parenting orders – including any possible restrictions for one parent (supervised, limited time, etc.). If possible, this could be done between the 2nd and 3rd sessions of Parent-Child Counseling, so that each parent could explain to the children the "new ways" of their family in the 3rd session. This provides stability, possible respect for each other, acceptance of new arrangements, and a possible end to the litigation. Depending on state requirements and court preferences, the parents would return to court to have their agreements approved or they could simply be filed with the court.

Step 4: Family (Or Court) Decision-Making

As described at the end of Step 3, it is possible that the parents will have reached some or all agreements regarding parenting by the end of the Individual and the Parent-Child Counseling. However, in many domestic violence cases, this will be unlikely. Therefore, they will go to court to argue their concerns and the court will make their decisions for them. This will occur somewhat differently in New Ways cases.

At the beginning of a full hearing on parenting issues (and possibly restraining orders and batterers' treatment orders, etc.), the judge will ask the parents what they have learned in their counseling sessions. This puts the emphasis learning skills for future behavior, rather than on defending past behavior.

Then, the judge will quiz each parent about a future parenting scenario similar to one described in the other parent's declaration about parenting concerns (see explanation of Behavioral Declarations in the New Ways description on the website). This puts the burden on each parent to convince the court that he or she would respond in an appropriate manner with the child/ren in the future, rather than focusing exclusively on past behavior.

Then, the judge could give the parties a tentative decision and encourage them to negotiate around it in the hallway with the assistance of their attorneys (if any), another professional or neutral family members.

Then, and only then, if they were unable to reach agreement on all issues (including parenting schedule, communication, future decision-making method, restraining orders, future batterers treatment or other treatment, parenting classes, etc.), they would proceed with an adversarial hearing or trial, with testimony and other evidence about past behavior. Also, at such a hearing, the court could call the Parent-Child Counselor to testify about what he or she observed between each parent and the children. The emphasis would be on specific questions that the court had about each parent's parenting skills, rather than on defending a Report, as the Parent-Child Counselor would not prepare a written report. This avoids shifting the focus to the "attack-defend" cycle that commonly occurs in high-conflict families around written reports.

Then, while the court will make findings about past behavior and orders which may restrict one parent, the court can emphasize areas of progress and the value of future treatment for one or both parents. The overall tone and focus of this Step 3 is future behavior change, rather than future re-litigation of the court's decisions.

Conclusion

New Ways for Families is a very new approach to high-conflict litigation, which appears likely to be helpful in handling domestic violence cases as well as other cases. However, this approach has not yet been tested on a significant sample and should be tried with caution by experienced professionals familiar with domestic violence cases and legal options.

Ideally, by putting structured counseling before decision-making, New Ways gives these families a chance to change, while also observing their ability to change. When in doubt, the court can order custody evaluations or psychological evaluations after the initial New Ways steps have helped contain the conflict and taught some basic skills. For some families, with Situational Couple Violence or Separation-Instigated Violence, this process may get them back on track for mostly positive parenting where there is a low risk for future violence. For other families, with Coercive Controlling Violence (and Violent Resistance in some cases), this approach may reduce the risks of direct parenting conflict and assist both parents in complying with restraining orders, treatment orders, and parenting restrictions.

CHAPTER 15
Dealing with Resistance

High-conflict people are highly defensive, so that negative feedback tends to trigger defensiveness rather than insight, and shuts down opportunities for teaching new skills. Therefore, working effectively with "resistance" to any feedback and criticism is one of the central issues of helping high-conflict people. Because of this defensiveness, they frequently deny that they have any problems and resist every effort that counselors and other professionals make to help them – even in their own self-interest.

Rather than engage in the usual "tug-of-war" with this resistance (which the clients are very used to), New Ways Counselors are encouraged to "dance" with the resistance, or to "go with the resistance" – by non-judgmentally exploring and discussing the client's concerns while providing information, rather than arguing with or confronting the client.

The following dialog is meant to help demonstrate these principles about resistance:

1) Don't argue with the client

2) Don't try to lead the client to have insights about his or her past behavior

3) Focus on helping the client learn to use the skills of New Ways in the future

4) The burden of solving the client's problems is always on the client, not the counselor

5) The counselor emphasizes giving information, giving choices and giving encouragement

In this example, Maria alleges that her husband, Javier, beat her up about 40 times during their 6-year marriage. Most recently, she got a scratch on her face and bruises on her arm, which she showed the judge when she obtained a restraining order - and an order for both parents to go through *New Ways for Families*. They have a son, Ray, age 5 years. Javier strongly denies any abusive behavior and believes that he should have primary physical custody and that Maria should have supervised access, as she takes medications for depression which he alleges cause her to fall down a lot and sleep a lot when she is supposed to be caring for Ray. Maria is seeking primary physical custody and wants supervised access for Javier with Ray just 2 hours a week.

The following dialog demonstrates some ways of dealing with resistance in this possible domestic violence case during a first session of *New Ways for Families*:

Counselor: I'm pleased to meet you Javier.

Javier: Well, I'm not pleased to meet you. I don't want to be here. I just want to see my son (5-year old Ray) and my wife.

Counselor: I see. I can certainly understand that. Now, you were ordered into this New Ways for Families program by the judge, correct?

Javier: Yes. The judge also ordered me to have no contact with my wife, Maria, or my son, Ray. He's 5 and he needs me. I should have custody of him, because his mother is always depressed and takes too much medication.

Counselor: Was that a temporary or permanent no contact order?

Javier: Temporary. Can you help me get to see my wife and son? Can you talk to the judge?

Counselor: Actually, I can't talk to the judge or to anyone else about your case. I'm not allowed to by court order. But I can help you learn some skills that might help you help yourself in your case.

Javier: I don't trust any of you guys. I've talked with counselors before and they just blame me for everything. You always believe the woman. I can't trust you at all.

Counselor: Well, I can understand that. You don't have to trust me. All you have to do in New Ways is learn some skills that you can use. And it's really up to you if you use them in the future. But you have to do the writing exercises in this workbook in order to get your Verification of Completion. That's what I sign once you've come to 6 sessions and done all the writing exercises.

Javier: I don't need to learn any skills. I just want to see my wife and my son.

Counselor: Well, actually learning these skills may help you see your wife and your son. The court usually wants to know that you are good enough at communicating and solving problems, before taking away no contact orders in a domestic violence case.

Javier: But I never hit my wife. What she said is a total lie.

Counselor: You might be right. I wasn't there, so I'll never know what happened. All I know is that she said on her Behavioral Declaration that you hit her up about 40 times during your 6-year marriage. So you'll need to deal with that statement somehow.

Javier: I just need to talk to Maria. She knows she lied and she'll realize she needs to tell the truth.

Counselor: You might be right. But for now it sounds like there's a restraining order not allowing any contact between you. So let's get started on this Parent Workbook so you can see if these skills will help you deal with your situation over the next 6 weeks. That's not too long, and you might find something useful in this - or not. It's up to you.

Javier: You keep saying it's up to me! But it isn't! Everyone else is telling me what to do.

Counselor: Using these skills is up to you. Filling out this workbook is up to you. Are you ready to get started?

Javier: Oh, all right!

[Workbook Pages 3-6: They talk about his goals for New Ways and hurdles that might get in the way of doing the writing. Javier reluctantly writes answers in his workbook. Then they talk about his strengths and positive qualities. He likes this part. Then he gives some background history of his family situation. Then, before his counselor talks about homework:]

Counselor: Now, before we talk about what to do in the coming week, there's a short, 5-minute statement I'm supposed to give you whenever someone alleges domestic violence in the family.

Javier: I told you: there's no domestic violence in our family – except for the couple times she's hit me.

Counselor: I understand. Like I said, you might be right. I'll never know and it really doesn't matter if I ever know. What matters in this counseling is that I teach you these skills and help you practice them so much that they're easy to do. And they might help you in court and with your son, too. So let me tell you about some patterns of domestic violence.

Javier: I'm not going to listen!

Counselor: Well, that part's up to you. I'm just required to tell you about these different types of domestic violence, so you'll know about them.

First, is what's called "battering," where a person hits the other person — and it could be a man or a woman, although its more often a man — from time to time throughout the relationship. It really is a pattern of behavior that doesn't change, unless the batterer practices different ways of solving problems over and over again. Sometimes, this pattern is based on wanting to feel connected to the person and not wanting to lose them. Other times, this pattern is based on wanting to control someone and no wanting to lose the feeling of control.

Javier: I'm not either of those types.

Counselor: Good! Even if you were, you could still change. It just takes a lot of practice, which can't really be done alone, so there's batterers treatment groups that help men change this behavior and help them have more successful relationships. I've had several clients go to one of these groups and they said they were really surprised at how much it helped them in every part of their lives. Even people who said they weren't batterers got a lot out of it. The judges often orders people into these programs if they have concerns that battering is going on in the family.

Anyway, there's a couple other types I want to tell you about. One is "situational violence" where there's pushing and shoving, maybe throwing things, because neither person knows how to stop an argument or resolve a conflict, so both get involved in this violent behavior.

Javier: That's Maria. She's attacked me a few times and then, when I push her away, she blames me for scratching her or bruising her arm. And you guys always think it's just my fault.

Counselor: Like I said, I'll never know. And the last kind is what they call "separation violence," when there's never been violence before, but there was an incident when the couple separated.

Javier: That last one might be what Maria was talking about when she got her restraining order. She was real upset and wanted to leave the house, but I could see that she might get into trouble if she tried to drive, so I held her arms to keep her from leaving until she calmed down. But she wiggled and fell down. That's when she scratched her face and bruised her arm. I was just trying to protect her from herself.

Counselor: Okay. Well, whatever the case, there are these patterns of battering and situational and separation violence, so that things will happen again in the future if you have one of those patterns. You can't just turn it off, without practicing new ways of managing problems. So if you have one of these patterns, you are encouraged to get some treatment in one of these groups. Otherwise, the judges often like to leave long-term restraining orders standing if they fear that these patterns will continue.

So that's my 5-minute statement about this. Do you have any questions?

Javier: No.

Counselor: Okay, then let's go to the next subject in the workbook. This is where we talk about homework for the coming week before our next meeting. All you have to do is see if you notice any all-or-nothing thinking, unmanaged emotions, and extreme behaviors in anyone. You don't even have to write these down.

Javier: That sounds stupid. Since I can't see Maria or Ray this week, I'm just going to be watching wrestling on TV. How can I look for all-or-nothing thinking with that?

Counselor: Well, you might notice if they just react, or if they seem to be thinking about their strategy and using flexible thinking in deciding their next move. Or notice if you think their behavior is extreme or moderate for the circumstances. Just notice everything around you and see if anyone does any of these three things: all-or-nothing thinking, unmanaged emotions, and extreme behaviors. Then we'll talk about it next week.

Javier: It still sounds stupid.

Counselor: That's okay. It's up to you whether you want to try noticing these things. You don't have to do any homework between sessions if you don't want to.

Javier: Good!

Counselor: Try to have a good week! See you next Tuesday.

Comment: following sessions will repeat the same general method of dealing with resistance by

1) trying to connect with the client around his concerns and
2) educating him about the realities of his possible situation.

The level at which he demonstrates learning the skills and applying them will help the court and/or other professionals determine his ability to change and future parenting arrangements. Some such clients may show a change in behavior and others will not. Therefore, this method of dealing with resistance is designed to maximize engagement with the client while not unrealistically assuming that all clients will learn and apply the skills in a positive fashion.

CHAPTER 16
Parent Workbooks

At the core of *New Ways for Families* are the Parent Workbooks:

Parent Workbook – for the Individual and Parent-Child Counseling in the full 12 week counseling model (Steps 2 & 3)

Or

Collaborative Parent Workbook – for the Individual and Parent-Child Coaching in the Collaborative Divorce Process (Steps 2 & 3)

Or

Decision Skills Workbook – Pre-Mediation Coaching Workbook - for the Pre-Mediation Coaching Model

The purpose of the workbooks is to open discussions with the counselors in a step-by-step manner. People with high-conflict personalities have been found to respond well to small steps, rather than expectations for large and dramatic changes of behavior. Based on the level of insight (or not) of each particular client, the therapist can use his or her skills to stretch the client's learning based on his or her abilities to reflect on and change his or her thinking, feelings and behavior.

In other words, the workbooks are not designed to be a comprehensive parenting course or a comprehensive treatment for abusive or alienating behavior. The goal is to stretch the parent's learning to give him or her new basic skills and a chance to change negative behaviors to the extent possible before negotiating or litigating long-term parenting plans.

Cognitive-Behavioral Approach

Using the workbooks helps reinforce the four basic lessons of flexible thinking, managed emotions, moderate behaviors and checking yourself. The entire process is designed to get parents thinking about their own behavior in a non-defensive way which may facilitate maximum learning. This "self-reflection" has been noted by many researchers as a missing process for high-conflict personalities.

Some people can be taught this skill, while others are too rigid and defensive to even consider it. It is most likely to be learned in a secure relationship with a counselor who can show empathy, provide a lot of validation for the person, and avoid getting emotionally hooked by the client's intense emotions. After Step 1 and Step 2, it should be more obvious to the court who can "self-reflect" and change their behavior, and who cannot.

Cognitive methods emphasize thinking and changing one's thinking. Written exercises are a key method in cognitive therapies. A great benefit of cognitive methods is that clients can do these written exercises at home and for years to come. A long-term relationship with a therapist is often less necessary when learning cognitive methods.

Behavioral methods emphasize trying new ways of doing things. In between sessions, clients are encouraged to try new behaviors that fit with the lessons of each session. General suggestions are contained in the workbooks, but specific behavioral exercises are to be based on discussions with the therapist.

In some ways it may appear that the workbooks are too easy and too general. However, when working with high-conflict personalities, small steps with a lot of validation are what is really needed to be effective. Large, dramatic changes are unlikely and counterproductive to attempt for many of these clients. Just as with treatments for addictions, the recovery process is on-going. The key is to see whether the person can "self-reflect" and begin to change in ways that will assist their children in growing up with flexible thinking, managed emotions, moderate behaviors and the ability to check themselves when new issues arise. The work of the therapist is to take the structure of the workbooks and build on them in each counseling session.

Articles Regarding Specific Parenting Behaviors

The workbooks have brief articles in the appendices, which offer suggestions for parenting behavior, negotiating techniques, and presenting information to the children. These articles relate to specific issues in the workbooks. Counselors are encouraged to read and discuss these articles with the clients in the course of the workbook exercises.

Writing in the Workbooks

Clients should complete the written assignments in the workbooks each session, either beforehand or during the session. Power struggles over homework are common with high-conflict clients and these can be avoided by allowing them to do the homework in the sessions. In some cases, the client will resist writing and ask the therapist to do the writing. If the client has a reading disability or resistance to writing is extremely high, the therapist could write what the client says. It must be the client's words for it to be effective. However, the client should be the one writing in the workbooks.

Storing the Workbooks

The Parent Workbook for the Individual Parent Counseling (Step 2) and the Parent-Child Counseling (Step 3) may be kept at the counselor's office, or taken home by the client. As the Individual Parent Counseling is confidential, this section of the Workbook should also be confidential. When the counseling has been completed, the client may keep the workbook or the workbook could be retained at the counselor's office as part of his or her confidential file. Or the client could discard the workbook. The choice should be the client's. Keep in mind that the client may return to the therapist in the future, either by his or her own request, or by a court order. However, in all cases, it should remain confidential regarding the Individual Parent Counseling.

Regarding the Parent-Child section of the Workbook, the reverse would be true. Since the Parent-Child Counseling is non-confidential, and since the counselor could be called to court to testify if the parents cannot make their own parenting plans, this section of the Workbook could also be required to be brought to court. The therapist should retain a copy of this section of the Workbook in his or her files, along with all other case records.

Obtaining the Workbooks

Therapists should read copies of the Workbooks before commencing the counseling process. Therapists may obtain multiple copies of the Workbooks from High Conflict Institute and/or clients may purchase them on their own from **www.NewWays4Families.com**.

The workbooks should be obtained by the parties or provided by the counselors <u>before</u> the first session of Individual Parent Counseling (so parent can prepare).

Based on the level of insight (or not) of each particular client, the therapist can use his or her skills to stretch the client's learning based on his or her abilities to reflect on and change his or her thinking, feelings and behavior.

CHAPTER 17
Starting a New Ways for Families Program

Any model is relatively easy to establish in any jurisdiction. In most court systems, judges already have the authority to order counseling when there is a parenting dispute. If not, they can still "encourage" the parents to get counseling, which may favorably impact their parenting orders after the counseling is completed.

Court-Based Counseling Model

There are four constituencies which must be included in planning to implement the Court-Based Counseling Model of the New Ways program:

- Judiciary
- Mental Health Professionals
- Attorneys
- Parents

Judiciary

Most judges immediately like the basic ideas of *New Ways for Families*. It is important to point out how New Ways may save them court time in the long run, especially as budgets are being cut and there may be a shortage of judicial officers. High-conflict families dominate family court calendars nationwide, so this may be a good time to approach the courts with the benefits to them of this new approach.

New Ways offers an opportunity for the courts to order counseling at the front end of potential high-conflict litigation, or at any time, from the time of separation to post-judgment litigation, when many of the worst parenting disputes occur. By ordering parents into New Ways, the court can delay high-conflict hearings and possibly eliminate them, if the parents learn skills which help them stay out of court and settle their own disputes.

It helps for the supervising judge in charge of family law to develop and approve basic procedures for the implementation of New Ways. Specifically, the court should approve the following three main documents, which may be distributed to attorneys, counselors and parents:

- Stipulation and Order that parties and courts may use
- List of trained New Ways Counselors and/ or agencies in the county/jurisdiction
- Parenting Instructions and the Behavioral Declaration and Reply Forms

In addition, it helps if the judiciary approves the following procedures:

- That parties and their attorneys, if any, may stipulate to use New Ways, using the Stipulation and Order.
- That a party may easily seek a court order for New Ways at a normal hearing or an ex parte (emergency) hearing.
- That normal parenting mediation or similar court programs may be postponed until after the New Way for Families Steps have been completed. This improves the likelihood that parents will settle their disputes and not need these services, or only need them once when they are most ready to settle.
- If the parties still need a court hearing after the counseling, the judge will:
- Quiz the parents on what they have learned in New Ways and quiz them on possible future parenting scenarios;
- THEN provide a tentative opinion about the case and encourage renewed settlement efforts, now that the parents see where the judge is headed;
- THEN, and only then, hear testimony and argument and make long-term court orders.

Training: At a minimum, judges should attend 1-3 hours of training for an overview of the *New Ways for Families* method, to become familiar with its basic differences from traditional counseling in family court cases. They need to understand the reasoning and procedures for each of the four steps. In particular, they need to understand the importance of using the basic Order for Counseling (New Ways), including the necessity and timing of deadlines, scheduling a hearing after the counseling, appointing the Parent-Child Counselor, respecting the confidentiality of the Individual Parent Counselors, limiting documents to the counselors to the Behavioral Declarations and Replies, and not having the Parent-Child Counselor write a report or make recommendations.

If possible, judges, mental health professionals, and attorneys should attend the 2-day training together so that they can meet each other, hear each others' questions, and support the same message of skills training and validation for parents. Ideally, at such a joint training session, the supervising judge or a delegated judge can explain how the court intends to use New Ways procedures in the specific county or jurisdiction.

High Conflict Institute offers all of the above training. See **www.NewWays4Families.com** for a schedule of trainings or contact us to request 1-2 days of training in your county/ jurisdiction.

Mental Health Professionals

The New Ways method is only as effective as the counselors who provide the counseling services. Ideally, all New Ways counselors should have several years of experience in handling high-conflict family court cases. High-conflict parents and high-conflict cases in the family courts have many predictable problems and there are many predictable interventions to use for the experienced counselor – often the opposite of what an inexperienced counselor might do.

With that said, some less-experienced counselors may be good therapists for the Individual Parent Counseling, especially those trained in cognitive-behavioral therapies. But the Parent-Child Counselor should be an experienced therapist with family court cases. Counselors can specify whether they would like to participate in New Ways as an Individual Counselor, or Parent-Child Counselor, or both. They all should take the 2-day training described below.

Training: Mental health professionals are required to complete the 2-day training in order to fully understand the structure of each step and to be listed as New Ways Counselors.

> Day 1 of the training covers Understanding and Managing High Conflict Personalities, the Research Basis for New Ways, the general structure and goals of New Ways, and training in handling specific high-conflict issues including domestic violence, child abuse and child alienation.

> Day 2 focuses on dealing with resistance with high-conflict people, an in-depth discussion of the structure of all four steps, and emphasizing practice exercises for each step.

High Conflict Institute offers all of the above training. See **www.NewWays4Families.com** for a schedule of trainings or contact us to request 1-2 days of training in your county/ jurisdiction.

New Ways Counselor List: A list of counselors who have been trained in using the New Ways method should be provided to the courts and may be listed on the New Ways website operated by High Conflict Institute. It should be noted if certain counselors only want to provide Individual Parent Counseling or only Parent-Child Counseling. If the program is being provided by a counseling agency instead of individual counselors, a list of these organizations should also be provided to the courts and may be listed on the New Ways website.

Sliding Fee Scale: When the program is provided by individual therapists, through their individual practice, it will significantly help promote the program if some therapists will volunteer to use a sliding fee scale for at least one out of every three New Ways cases that they take. When provided by counseling agencies, a sliding scale similar to the one in place for other counseling services within the agency is recommended. Judges and court counselors/mediators will hesitate to refer parents to this program if it appears unaffordable for their clients.

Attorneys

It is essential that attorneys understand and support all four steps of *New Ways for Families*. Attorneys are often the first professional contact that a potentially high-conflict parent has with the legal system. Many of these parents really want to fight in family court and will have little interest in using *New Ways for Families*. Therefore, attorneys will need to see the value of this program to their clients and to themselves.

Benefit to clients: Most high-conflict clients do not view themselves as having any problems. They are preoccupied with the other parent's behavior. They do not need to be confronted with their own behavior. They just need to understand that this method can help them deal with the other parent, no matter how difficult the other parent may be. Also, volunteering for this program is an effective way of getting the other parent into counseling. Parents who are already reasonable will appreciate the additional skills for handling the other parent.

Benefit to attorneys: Most attorneys are frustrated with their high-conflict clients, or are frustrated with their cases in which there is a high-conflict party on the other side. They often wish these cases would go away, or that there was some way to contain the conflict. New Ways is a good alternative for them, as it will contain both parties with a structure and a counselor for each party to talk to about the separation or divorce. This should reduce the crisis phone calls from their client and from the opposing party or attorney. The New Ways method may also make it easier to reach a settlement and make preparing for court with a difficult client unnecessary.

Training: It is highly recommended that attorneys complete 1- 2 days of New Ways training, in order to understand the four steps, the procedures, and how it differs from traditional counseling. In particular, attorneys need to understand that the Individual Parent Counselor cannot talk to the attorney and that the counselor should not receive any documents other than the Behavioral Declarations and the Reply Behavioral Declarations and related parenting orders. This may also help them understand what their clients are going through and how they can support the overall process.

High Conflict Institute offers all of the above training. See **www.NewWays4Families.com** for a schedule of trainings or contact us to request 1-2 days of training in your county/jurisdiction.

New Ways Lawyer List: Some attorneys may wish to be on a list of New Ways-trained attorneys, which the court may provide to parents and which may be posted on the New Ways website. Some attorneys may also wish to be listed as willing to assist self-representing parties on an hourly consulting basis. This is a good option for clients who don't want to commit to the ongoing cost of a retained attorney, and a good option for attorneys whose consulting work may occasionally turn in to full cases.

Parents

Parents themselves are a key part of promoting the use of *New Ways for Families*. Reasonable parents may immediately see the benefit of this method as a way to get their high-conflict spouse or partner into counseling. Parents who are alleged to have abused or alienated a child, or abused a spouse, may see this as a way to demonstrate changes in their own parenting behavior before long-term orders are made restricting their parenting (no contact, supervised visitation, limited parenting time).

Informing parents about New Ways: Parents may be informed through handouts at their attorney's or therapist's office, through handouts provided at court, or through short articles in local papers. If there is a sliding fee scale, they should be informed about that, as it may make a difference in whether they seek this method or reject it. They should be informed that they can both stipulate to New Ways without having to ask a judge to order it. If one parent resists using this method, then an individual parent needs to know the procedures for acquiring a court order for the program. Parents can be encouraged to "Ask for New Ways!"

Parent Handouts: As described above, there should be a brief handout explaining the basic benefits and procedures of *New Ways for Families*. In addition, there should be a brief handout of "Parent Instructions" once New Ways has been ordered. This would primarily tell the parent about the detailed steps and what each parent must do during each of those steps. These handouts can be obtained from High Conflict Institute at the address in the front of this Guidebook.

Other Models:

New Ways for Families can also be implemented in any of the alternative models, even without significant court participation. However, it's important to note that potentially high-conflict parents often will not participate in helping themselves, unless coerced to do so by a court order or other negative consequence.

For more information on implementing one of the other models, please contact *New Ways for Families* at **www.NewWays4Families.com** or (619) 221-9108. There are many training options available, including a live training, training via DVD, training via Skye, or a combination of these training methods. The content of the training is applicable to any family law professional interested in working with New Ways, including: judges, attorneys, mediators, therapists and other mental health professionals, parenting coordinators and parent educators. All training requires at least three participants, in order effectively work through the practice exercises.

Materials

All of the materials necessary to start a *New Ways for Families* program in your jurisdiction can be obtained from the New Ways website, operated by High Conflict Institute. Here are the basic materials:

Pre-Mediation Coaching Workbook: Instructions and lessons for the Pre-Mediation Coaching model.

Professional Guidebook: Instructions and reasoning for all professionals involved, including judges, lawyers and mental health professionals. Includes sample forms.

Parent Workbook: Instructions, lessons, and related articles for the six Individual Parent Counseling sessions and the three Parent-Child Counseling sessions.

Collaborative Workbook: Instructions, lessons, and related articles for the three Individual Parent Coaching sessions and the three Parent-Child Coaching sessions.

Decisions Skills Workbook: Instructions and lessons for the Decisions Skills Class model.

Instructor's Manual: Instructions and articles related to the Decisions Skills Class model.

Sample Court Orders: Blank court orders which can be filled in and used, so long as approved in the specific county/jurisdiction, are available on the website. An example court order with blanks filled in. [See Appendix I of this Guidebook.]

Website Listing Form: Listing Form, as part of the New Ways Network [See Appendix IV of this Guidebook.] Professionals may specify what information from this form they want listed on the website.

Sample Behavioral Declarations & Instructions: Blank Behavioral Declarations, blank Reply Behavioral Declarations available on the website. Examples of each. [See Appendix III of this Guidebook.]

Parent Brochure: Basic information about New Ways for Families for parents.

Training

All of the training necessary to start a *New Ways for Families* program in your jurisdiction can be obtained from High Conflict Institute, **www.NewWays4Families.com**. Several training options are available, including training via Skype and DVD. Please contact New Ways to discuss training options.

Standard training is as follows:

Basic Training, Judges: Minimum 1-hour overview of the 4-step method, research basis, Sample Court Order, and differences from traditional counseling in family court cases. Ideally, judges would attend Day 1 of the 2-day training, with lawyers and therapists.

Basic Training for Lawyers: 3-6 hour overview of the 4-step method, handling special issues (domestic violence, child abuse, child alienation, false allegations), research basis, New Ways forms, Parent Workbooks, explaining program to clients, supporting client during program, cognitive-behavioral assignments, dealing with resistance in high-conflict cases, and negotiating settlement as much as possible.

Training for Therapists: 2-day training required for therapists. Day 1 is a 6-hour seminar focusing on the dynamics of personality disorders (traits of which most often drive high-conflict cases), analysis of the general conflict and litigation and negotiation behaviors of these personality types, ten skills for managing high-conflict people, and ethical issues common in high-conflict disputes. This is a good introduction for all professionals who work with high-conflict clients and for all of those who will be working with New Ways clients. Day 2 is a 6-hour seminar consisting of an in-depth discussion of the structure of the four steps, including practice exercises.

Conclusion

New Ways for Families is a new method for family courts. This Professional Guidebook is a work in progress and will be adapted over time, based on real life experience. Self-reflection and change are central to the messages contained in the New Ways method, so it is appropriate for these principles to be practiced in the use of this method.

Any court system can try this method at any time. However, the success of this method relies primarily on the skill of the practitioners who use it. Therefore, we highly recommend that practitioners be trained in this method by our High Conflict Institute trainers.

Contact us at **www.NewWays4Families.com** for information about training dates, locations and fees.

Technical assistance from High Conflict Institute is available to implement *New Ways for Families* in your community or jurisdiction.

This is a totally new method for family courts, although it is based on principles derived from well-established programs in other settings. We intend to research the effectiveness of this method in the future and we are very interested in your experiences with it. Please contact us with your feedback and questions at **info@newways4families.com**.

Best wishes in the work ahead!

APPENDIX I:
Court Order Instructions
& Sample Court Order

INSTRUCTIONS FOR COURT ORDERS (NEW WAYS)

The attached Court Order for Counseling (New Ways) is designed to give parents, counselors and attorneys complete instructions for the *New Ways for Families* method. Each step has been carefully designed to contain and reduce unnecessary conflict, while helping each parent focus on strengthening their own skills for parenting, dealing with the other parent, and making decisions. It gives parents clear deadlines to complete each step of the process. You are encouraged to use this order as written as much as possible. Following are some specific explanations to assist with the order:

Findings: First, parents and their lawyers, if any, should be encouraged to stipulate to this counseling method, so that they will be more committed. However, if one or both parties object, the court should proceed to make the necessary findings under state and local rules to allow for court-ordered counseling.

Individual Parent Counselor: Each parent should choose a counselor trained in the New Ways method from the current court list or from **www.NewWays4Families.com**. The Individual Parent Counseling is designed to be totally confidential, so the client can focus solely on counseling rather than trying to engage the counselor in the court action.

Parent-Child Counselor: **The court should name the Parent-Child Counselor in the order** from the current court list or from **www.NewWays4Families.com**. This counselor should be someone with substantial family court experience. This counselor does not write a report or make any recommendations, but may testify about observations of the parents with their children, so long as the parents sign proper releases.

Interim Hearing Date: In cases in which temporary No Contact or Supervised Visitation has been ordered, an interim hearing can take place after the first 6 weeks of Individual Parent Counseling to re-evaluate whether the temporary order should be revised.

Efforts to Settle or Mediate: The parents should be encouraged to settle all of their parenting issues after the New Ways counseling, as they should have more skills and motivation. If possible, the use of court-required mediation (FCS) should occur after rather than before the counseling. A hearing date should be set to provide motivation, which could be cancelled later.

Recommended Deadlines for New Ways Court Orders:

The date the order is issued is "Day 1":

> #4. Individual Counseling completed by
> _____ [7 weeks after Day 1]

#5.   Interim Hearing Date (if needed—see above)
_____ [8 weeks after Day 1]

#10. Parent-Child Counseling completed by
_____ [13 weeks after Day 1]

#12. Court mediation completed by
_____ [14 weeks after Day 1]

#13. Next court hearing on
_____ [18 weeks after Day 1]

**TELL PARENTS TO CALL NEW WAYS OFFICE
FOR INSTRUCTIONS 619-209-7796.**

--- SAMPLE COURT ORDER ---

The following is a Sample Case Example of the Court Order. Blank Court Orders can be found on the New Ways website. State laws and local rules should be reviewed for the applicability of this counseling order. High Conflict Institute, LLC does not warrant that this order is sufficient or appropriate for use in any specific state.

SUPERIOR COURT OF THE STATE OF CALIFORNIA
FOR THE COUNTY OF SAN DIEGO

In re the Matter of:	Case No. D 9119111
Petitioner: SARA TURELL	COURT ORDER FOR COUN-SELING ("NEW WAYS") UNDER FC§3190
and	
Respondent: BRAD TURELL	DATE: January 28, 2009 TIME: 9:00am DEPT: F-27

_____ Based upon the agreement of the parties, the court hereby makes the following Orders:

__✔__Upon good cause shown, the court hereby makes the following Findings and Orders:

FINDINGS (Not necessary if agreement by the parties):

1. The dispute between the parents poses a substantial danger to the best interest of the child, and counseling is in the best interest of the child, for the following reason(s):

_____ Mother is requesting restricted parenting for Father _____.

2. The financial burden created by this court order for counseling does not otherwise jeopardize a party's other financial obligations, because of the following reason(s):

_____ Both parents' financial forms show sufficient income for this counseling _____.

INDIVIDUAL PARENT COUNSELING

1. Mother and father shall each participate in six (6) counseling sessions of 45-60 minutes each with a licensed mental health professional using

the *New Ways for Families Parent Workbook.* Each parent shall contact a separate Individual Parent Counselor trained in the New Ways method within seven (7) days. When the six (6) sessions have been completed and the Parent Workbook has been completed, each parent shall provide a copy of their counselor's signed Verification of Completion to the court and the opposing party/attorney.

2. The Individual Parent Counseling described above shall be paid for by:

__✔__ Each parent shall pay for his or her own counseling.

_____ Father/Mother shall pay the cost of the counseling for both parents.

_____ Father/Mother shall advance the cost of the counseling for both parents, reserving the final allocation of the cost to the court.

3. The Individual Parent Counseling described above shall be Confidential. The Individual Parent Counselor shall never submit any letter, declaration or document (other than the Verification of Completion of the Individual Parent Counseling) to the court, nor testify in court, subject to rare exceptions by law. Said Counselor shall not communicate with any other professional involved in the case, except by written agreement of both parties after each has attended at least 4 sessions.

4. The counseling described above shall be completed by: March 18, 2009.

5. Interim Hearing Date (if temporary No Contact or Supervised Parenting orders):

March 25, 2009_____.

PARENT-CHILD COUNSELING

6. Mother and father shall each participate in three (3) parent-child counseling sessions with their child/ren of 45-90 minutes each with a shared licensed mental health professional using the New Ways for Families Parent Workbook. The parties shall specifically use: __Mr. Desjardins__ as their Parent-Child Counselor or a Parent-Child Counselor selected by the parties/counsel trained in the New Ways method.

7. The parents shall alternate Parent-Child Counseling Sessions approximately each week. Both parents shall complete Session #1, before either parent attends Session #2. Both parents shall complete Session #2, before either parent attends Session #3. When the three (3) sessions have been completed and the Parent-Child Counseling section of the Parent

Workbook has been completed by each parent, he or she shall provide a copy of their Parent-Child Counselor's signed Verification of Completion to the court and to the opposing party/attorney.

8. The Parent-Child Counseling described above shall be paid for by:

    __✔__ Each parent shall pay for his or her own counseling.

    _____ Father/Mother shall pay the cost of the counseling for both parents.

    _____ Father/Mother shall advance the cost of the counseling for both parents, reserving the final allocation of the cost to the court.

9. The Parent-Child Counseling described above shall be Non-Confidential, subject to state laws. The counselor may discuss the case with the Attorney of Record for each party, Minor's Counsel, a jointly selected Mediator, an appointed High-Conflict Case Manager, and/or Collaborative Team members. The Parent-Child Counselor may be called to testify, describe observations, and produce counseling records, if called as a witness by either party or the court, subject to the court's discretion. The counselor shall not submit a written report or recommendations. The counselor shall not serve as an expert in the case.

10. The counseling described above shall be completed by: April 29, 2009 .

DOCUMENTS FOR COUNSELORS

11. Each parent shall provide a 2-page Behavioral Declaration and a 2-page Reply Behavioral Declaration to the other party and to his or her Individual Parent Counselor and the Parent-Child Counselor, along with copies of all related parenting Court Orders, including this Order, at least two business days prior to the first day of counseling. Each party shall provide copies of the other parent's Behavioral Declaration and Reply Behavioral Declaration to his or her Individual Parent Counselor promptly upon receipt. Neither party shall provide any additional court documents to the counselors. The counselors shall not request any additional court documents. Each party shall provide copies of his or her own Behavioral Declaration and Reply Behavioral Declaration to the Parent-Child Counselor at least ten calendar days prior to the first day of either party's Parent-Child Counseling.

NEXT HEARING

12. Whether or not both parties have completed the counseling described above, there shall be a Family Court Services or private recommending mediation by ___May 6, 2009___ .

13. There shall be a hearing on ___June 3, 2009___ , unless the parties have reached a full, written agreement on all issues before the court.

PARENT INSTRUCTIONS

14. The parents shall immediately contact the New Ways for Families office to obtain instructions, current referral lists and to answer any questions at 619-209-7796.

THE FOREGOING IS STIPULATED TO BY:

Date _____   _____N/A_____

Date _____   _____ N/A_____

Date _____   _____N/A_____

Date _____   _____ N/A_____

IT IS SO ORDERED:

Date: _____

___Alan B. Clements___

Judge of the Superior Court

APPENDIX II:
Out-of-Court
Agreement

Agreement to Use
New Ways for Families

We, the undersigned, hereby agree to use the *New Ways for Families* method to help our children develop resilience and to help us with our parenting plan.

We agree to the following specific terms:

1. To participate in at least six Individual Counseling sessions which are focused on the material and exercises provided in the New Ways for Families' Parent Workbook.

2. To obtain our workbooks prior to the first Individual Parent Counseling session, to write all of the exercises in the New Ways Parent Workbook when instructed, and to discuss them with our Counselors.

3. To complete the six New Ways Individual Parent Counseling sessions by _____.

4. To participate in at least three Parent-Child Counseling sessions with our child/ren which are focused on the material and exercises provided in the Parent Workbook.

5. To complete the three New Ways Parent-Child Counseling meetings by _____.

6. That the New Ways Individual Parent Counseling Sessions shall be **confidential** from all professionals and the court, subject to state law reporting requirements.

7. That the New Ways Parent-Child Counseling Sessions are intended to be **non-confidential** among professionals and the court, subject to the understanding that this is a voluntary decision and that separate signed releases are still necessary.

8. To make our best efforts to use **flexible thinking, managed emotions,** and **moderate behaviors** in our communication with each other, in making our decisions and in parenting our children.

Signature: _____

Name: _____

Date: _____

Signature: _____

Name: _____

Date: _____

[For cases without a court order]   *Revd 7/2011*

APPENDIX III:
Parent Instructions &
Sample Behavioral Declarations

PARENT INSTRUCTIONS

DEAR PARENT:

You are going to be using *New Ways for Families*, a new method for handling separation and divorce issues. New Ways is designed to provide you and your children with skills for resilience during this time of significant change in your family, before making big decisions. It does not require you to have contact with the other parent at any time, however that is an option. New Ways has 4 basic steps:

Step 1: Getting Started, which includes signing a stipulation to participate in New Ways and/or getting a court order to participate in New Ways, including the appointment of a Parent-Child Counselor.

- Go to **www.NewWays4Families.com** and click on **"For Families"** where you will find everything you need to complete this program, including Forms and Instructions.
- First, select and contact an Individual Parent Counselor of your choosing from the New Ways Counselor List.
- Second, print and complete the Behavioral Declaration Form (instructions available on the website)
- Purchase the Parent Workbook

Step 2: Individual Counseling, which includes 6 sessions with your own <u>confidential</u> counselor. Take the Parent Workbook he Parent Workbook This counseling includes a Parent Workbook, which you will write in during your sessions and possibly before and after your sessions.

Step 3: Parent-Child Counseling, which includes 3 sessions each with you and your child/ren (alternating weeks with the other parent over 6 weeks). You and the other parent share the same <u>non-confidential</u> counselor. You will each have your own Parent Workbook for these sessions. This counselor does not write a report or make recommendations, but can report observations to the court, if necessary.

Step 4: Family (or Court) Decision-making, which includes settlement negotiations for a new parenting plan with the assistance of professionals if possible, such as attorneys or a mediator. If you are unable to settle the case, then the court will make decisions for you at your next hearing.

BEST WISHES!

BEHAVIORAL DECLARATIONS
INSTRUCTIONS

Behavioral Declarations provide your New Ways Counselors with brief information about the three most serious concerns each parent has about the other's parenting skills. Reply Behavioral Declarations indicate whether each parent agrees or not with the concerns of the other. These help the counselors help the parents, by knowing the issues from each parent's point of view, and how much agreement or disagreement there is.

These are the only declarations which may be seen by the New Ways Counselors in your case. In preparing these two declarations, you are encouraged to seek the assistance of a lawyer trained in *New Ways for Families*, to help you provide the most useful information and possibly to help settle your case. A list of lawyers trained in New Ways is available at **www.NewWays4Families.com** or 619-209-7796 or ask your lawyer.

The following instructions will help you prepare these declarations:

A) **What to write in your Behavioral Declaration:** See the first attached blank form for headings about what to write. You can use this form. It should be no longer than 2 pages. Your Behavioral Declaration should describe specific behaviors that are a concern for you about the other parent, strengths of the other parent, and what you are requesting regarding parenting plans.

B) **Provide to Individual Counselor 2 business days before your counseling begins:** Behavioral Declarations and any related parenting court orders should be provided to your Individual Parent Counselor at least 2 business days before your first counseling session. A copy of your Behavioral Declaration should also be provided at least 2 business days before your first session to the other parent (to give to his or her Individual Parent Counselor).

C) **What to write in your REPLY Behavioral Declaration:** See the second attached blank form for headings about what to write. This should be only 2 pages. Explain whether you Agree or Disagree (and why not) with what the other parent's concerns are about your parenting behavior, and any changes in your requests regarding parenting plans.

D) **Provide 5 business days after receiving other parent's Behavioral Declaration:** REPLY Behavioral Declarations should be provided to your Individual Parent Counselor no more than 5 business days after you receive the other parent's Behavioral Declaration. A copy of your REPLY Behavioral Declaration should also be provided on the same day to the other parent (to give to his or her Individual Parent Counselor).

E) **Provide to Parent-Child Counselor 10 calendar days before Parent-Child Counseling begins:** Provide your Behavioral Declaration, your Reply Behavioral Declaration and any related parenting court orders to the Parent-Child Counselor at least 10 calendar days before your first Parent-Child Counseling session.

F) **Do Not File With Court:** The purpose of these declarations is to inform the counselors of your concerns, strengths, agreements or disagreements, and requests. They should not be filed with the court. Consult with an attorney if you have any questions.

WILLIAM BENJAMIN
Attorney at Law
P. O. Box 70067
San Diego, California 92167
Telephone: (619) 555-1234
Facsimile: (619) 555-1235

Attorney for SARA TURELL

[SAMPLE]

SUPERIOR COURT OF THE STATE OF CALIFORNIA
FOR THE COUNTY OF SAN DIEGO

In re the Matter of:	**Case No. 911911**
SARA TURELL	**BEHAVIORAL DECLARATION OF SARA TURELL**
and	
BRAD TURELL	

Date of Marriage/Living Together: October 1, 1997

Date of Separation: January 3, 2009

Children's names and dates of birth: Thomas Turell, DOB: October 17, 1999

Tara Turell, DOB: May 11, 2002

MOTHER'S 3 STRONGEST CONCERNS ABOUT FATHER'S PARENTING

1. On January 18, 2009, Brad hit our son, Tommy, age 10, with a belt on his buttocks, because Tommy would not do his homework. Brad did this once before two years ago. Each time he was arguing with Tommy about doing his homework. Tommy was tearful when he described this to me after the weekend at his father's. I called Brad and tried to discuss this with him, but he told me to mind my own business. I am concerned that he will do this again and again, now that I am not around when he has the children.

2. On January 24, 2009, Brad came to our house (he had not been served with the TRO yet). He pounded on the front screen door, yelling that he wanted to see his children. He pounded so hard that the screen door fell off its hinge. The children and I were frightened for our lives. I called the

police. They came and issued a 5-day protective order. They told him to leave immediately and he did.

3. On several occasions over the years, including one month before we separated, Brad told Tommy that he has to spend time on a woodworking project with his father. When Tommy shows that he is not interested, his father still requires him to do this. Tommy feels pressured to do these projects and I am concerned that he will just go along with his father and not be allowed to develop his academic interests in my absence. Brad is a janitor with a high school education, while I have a Master's Degree.

II. MOTHER'S VIEW OF FATHER'S 3 BEST STRENGTHS

1. Brad encourages Tommy to stick up for himself if anyone picks on him at school.

2. When Tommy was 9, Brad took him on a camping trip with two other friends and their sons. He taught Tommy how to tie different kinds of knots.

3. Brad wants Tommy and Tara to go to college after they graduate high school.

III.   MOTHER'S PARENTING REQUESTS

1. I strongly request that the court make the Temporary Restraining Orders permanent, so that Brad stays away from my house and from the children, except during his supervised parenting time. He has said that he can come over whenever he wants to.

2. I would like Brad to have supervised visitation with Tommy, to protect him from being hit with a belt. I would like this supervised visitation to occur during the daytime on Saturdays. The rest of the time Tommy would be with me.

3. Brad should have to attend a parenting class and an anger management class.

Date: 1/30/09   Sara Turell

SARA TURELL, Petitioner

There should be no attachments. Provide this to your Individual Counselor and the other parent, after you receive the other parent's Behavioral Declaration. This should not be filed with the court.

BRAD TURELL
In Propia Persona
123 Maple Street
San Diego, California 92103
Telephone: (619) 123-4567

Attorney for BRAD TURELL, In Propia Persona

[SAMPLE]

SUPERIOR COURT OF THE STATE OF CALIFORNIA
FOR THE COUNTY OF SAN DIEGO

In re the Matter of:	Case No. 911911
SARA TURELL	**BEHAVIORAL DECLARATION OF**
and	**BRAD TURELL**
BRAD TURELL	

Date of Marriage/Living Together: October 1, 1997

Date of Separation: January 3, 2009

Children's names and dates of birth: Thomas Turell, DOB: October 17, 1999

Tara Turell, DOB: May 11, 2002

FATHER'S 3 STRONGEST CONCERNS ABOUT MOTHER'S PARENTING

1. On three different days, before I moved out, Sara told the children that the divorce "is all your father's fault." She also yelled at me in front of the children that they "would be better off if they never saw their father again." The children seemed very uncomfortable after she said these things.

2. She called Child Protective Services on me when I hit Tommy with my belt. I did that two years ago, and she did nothing. I am convinced that she will do anything to push me out of the children's lives and get her way.

3. She cries a lot in front of the children and it worries them. Then they blame it on me. But it's her own fault. She makes herself upset. She's very dramatic and I'm afraid it will affect the children if they spend too

much time with her.

FATHER'S VIEW OF MOTHER'S 3 BEST STRENGTHS

1. Sara is good at shopping for the children. She knows what looks good on them.
2. Sara is better at helping them with their homework, but I am learning.
3. Sara wants Tommy and Tara to go to college after they graduate high school.

FATHER'S PARENTING REQUESTS

1. I would like to have the restraining order removed. I have never hit Sara and she has never claimed I did. I will not hit Tommy with a belt again. This only happened two times ever. My father did that with me and now it is clear it is not allowed anymore.
2. I would like to have the children 50% of the time. I had more than that while Sara was getting her Master's degree.
3. I would like Sara to get some counseling, as she cries and yells a lot.

Date: 1/30/09   ___BRAD Turell___

BRAD TURELL, Respondent

There should be no attachments. Provide this to your Individual Counselor and the other parent, after you receive the other parent's Behavioral Declaration. This should not be filed with the court.

WILLIAM BENJAMIN
Attorney at Law
P. O. Box 70067
San Diego, California 92167
Telephone: (619) 555-1234
Facsimile: (619) 555-1235

Attorney for SARA TURELL

[SAMPLE]

SUPERIOR COURT OF THE STATE OF CALIFORNIA
FOR THE COUNTY OF SAN DIEGO

In re the Matter of:	**Case No. 911911**
SARA TURELL	**REPLY BEHAVIORAL DECLARA-**
and	**TION OF SARA TURELL**
BRAD TURELL	

MOTHER'S AGREEMENT/DISAGREEMENT WITH FATHER'S CONCERNS

1. Father's Concern #1: I agree that I said the divorce was Brad's fault and that the children would be better off if they never saw him again. But I was telling them the truth, which is very important to me. I want the children to grow up being very honest.

2. Father's Concern #2: Two years ago, after Brad hit Tommy with his belt the first time, I told him to never do it again. I didn't call Child Protective Services then, because I didn't know about them then. He didn't do it again until we separated. Now I'm more concerned it will happen again and again.

3. Father's Concern #3: I do not agree that I cry and yell a lot in front of the children. Divorce is an upsetting time and anyone would cry and yell some. I do not believe that I am any more emotional than anyone else would be and I do not need counseling.

II: REVISED PARENTING REQUESTS: None

Date: 2/4/09   <u>   Sara Turell   </u>

SARA TURELL, Petitioner

There should be no attachments. Provide this to your Individual Counselor and the other parent, after you receive the other parent's Behavioral Declaration. This should not be filed with the court.

BRAD TURELL
In Propia Persona
123 Maple Street
San Diego, California 92103
Telephone: (619) 123-4567

Attorney for THOMAS TURELL, In Propia Persona

[SAMPLE]

SUPERIOR COURT OF THE STATE OF CALIFORNIA
FOR THE COUNTY OF SAN DIEGO

In re the Matter of:

SARA TURELL	**Case No. 911911**
and	**REPLY BEHAVIORAL DECLARA-**
BRAD TURELL	**TION OF BRAD TURELL**

I. FATHER'S AGREEMENT/DISAGREEMENT WITH MOTHER'S CONCERNS

1. Mother's Concern #1: I agree that I hit Tommy with my belt when he wouldn't do his homework last month. I agree that I should not do that. I did that once two years ago, and no one called it abuse or called Child Protective Services. Now that it is clearly not allowed, I will never do it again. I have never been accused of abusing our children before. When I picked up the children that weekend, Sara made a big fuss about making sure that Tommy did his homework. I felt a lot of pressure to get him to do it. I shouldn't have let her get to me that way and I don't think it will ever happen again.

2. Mother's Concern #2: I do not agree that I was threatening Sara's and the children's lives when I was knocking on the front screen door. It has been in need of repair for a long time, so it was not surprising that it fell off its hinge. I was frustrated that she was not answering the door. I did not know about the restraining order and left right away when the police gave it to me. I do not think that I need an anger management class.

3. Mother's Concern #3: I do not agree that I pressure Tommy to do wood-working projects with me. He really enjoys doing them with me. It's some-thing I have to offer him, even though I do not have as much education as their mother. When he does not want to work on woodworking, I let him do something else.

II. REVISED PARENTING REQUESTS

I would like to add that Sara should be ordered to tell the children that she was not in fear for her life when I knocked on the door. She has never been afraid of me and never before accused me of any abuse of her or the chil-dren, except for the belt incident. This is another example of her exaggerated crying and yelling.

I declare under penalty of perjury under the laws of the State of California that the foregoing is true and correct.

Date: 2/5/09   __BRAD Turell__

BRAD TURELL, Respondent

There should be no attachments. Provide this to your Individual Counselor and the other parent, after you receive the other parent's Behavioral Declara-tion. This should not be filed with the court.

APPENDIX IV:
New Ways for Families
Network

New Ways for Families Network of Professionals

New Ways for Families maintains a Network of professionals who have completed the New Ways training. Professionals and organizations who join the Network will be listed on the New Ways website as a New Ways-provider, will receive discounts on New Ways materials, and will receive a newsletter for professionals, with comments, tips, suggestions, and success stories from other jurisdictions. High Conflict Institute and *New Ways for Families* provide consultation services for Network professionals as well.

New Ways for Families Counselor Referral Lists

Counselors who wish to join the New Ways Network and be listed on the website must satisfy the following requirements:

(1) complete the required training, depending the model to be used;

(2) complete the Licensing Agreement and New Ways Website Listing Form; and

(3) provide a copy of a current license and current malpractice insurance.

The terms of the Licensing Agreement vary depending on the intent of use and needs of the organization, professional, or community. Please contact us to discuss appropriate adaptation of the Licensing Agreement.

The Listing Form includes a questionnaire allowing each professional to specify their preferences for participating in the New Ways Program. Counselors may specify whether they would like to participate as an Individual Parent Counselor, Parent-Child Counselor, or both, and whether they will be offering a sliding fee scale for New Ways clients. Those who would like to participate as a Parent-Child Counselor must have significant family court experience. Counselors may also specify whether they are interested in taking cases with domestic violence allegations. Counselors wishing to do so must have significant experience with domestic violence cases.

New Ways for Families Lawyer & Mediator Referral Lists

Lawyers and mediators may wish to be listed on the website as a resource for parents who are looking for family law professionals familiar with the program. After completing the training and the website listing form, lawyers and mediators can be listed on the website as trained in the New Ways method. Lawyers and mediators are not required to complete a Licensing Agreement or provide a copy of their license and malpractice insurance, as they are not actually providing the therapy.

On the Website Listing Form, lawyers can specify whether they are interested in taking cases for representation, or for consultation on an hourly basis, or both, and whether they will be offering a free one-half hour consultation for New Ways clients. Lawyers can also specify whether they are interested in taking cases with domestic violence allegations.

APPENDIX V:
Coordination Letter &
Verifications of Completion

NEW WAYS FOR FAMILIES
COORDINATION LETTER

Dear New Ways Parent-Child Counselor _____:

I have attended my first New Ways Individual Counseling session. I agree to participate in six sessions of New Ways Individual Counseling, then to participate in three sessions of New Ways Parent-Child Counseling.

1. My contact information is as follows:

Full name: _____

Phone (circle: Cell/Home/Work):_____

Second Phone, if any (Cell/Home/Work): _____

Mailing address: _____

_____

_____

2. My Individual Counselor's name is _____.

    I understand that you will not be talking to my Individual Counselor, as the New Ways Individual Counselor is confidential, unless after the sixth session I choose to allow him or her to speak with you. I understand that decision is totally up to me. I expect to complete my six Individual Counseling sessions by

    _____.

3. I understand that I cannot do the New Ways Parent-Child Counseling until both parents have completed our New Ways Individual Counseling. I will contact you after my fifth or sixth Individual Counseling session to schedule the start of my Parent-Child Counseling.

4. I understand that you, as the Parent-Child Counselor, will not be confidential and can talk to our lawyers (if any), to Family Court Services (FCS), to the judge, and others, so long as I sign a release for you to do so, in the event that we do not settle our case out of court.

5. I agree/do not agree to "continue" any hearings for long-term parenting decisions until all of these counseling sessions are completed, including postponing Family Court Services. FCS is scheduled for _____which I plan to: attend/postpone (circle one). A Court Hearing is scheduled for _____ which I plan to: attend/postpone.

6. ___ I am enclosing my Behavioral Declaration about the other parent's parenting.

   ___ I am enclosing copies of all current court orders related to counseling and parenting.

   ___ I am enclosing my Reply Behavioral Declaration. (Received other's Reply? Yes/ No)

Date: _____   Signature:_____

Client Name _____

Case Number_____

VERIFICATION OF COMPLETION OF NEW WAYS FOR FAMILIES: INDIVIDUAL COUNSELING

Date first contacted by parent______________________________

Date Received Parent's Behavioral Declaration ____________________

Date Received copy of court orders from parent____________________

Date Received Parent's Reply Declaration________________________

Date Parent attended 1st Individual Session ______________________

Upon completion, the Individual Counselor should copy this sheet, sign it and submit it to the client. The client may provide it to anyone he or she chooses, including other professionals and/or the court.

I hereby verify that __________________________ has attended at least 6 sessions of New Ways for Families: Individual Counseling of at least 45 minutes each. I hereby verify that he or she has completed all of the corresponding written assignments for 6 sessions of New Ways Individual Counseling.

I believe it would be appropriate/inappropriate (circle one) for this client to proceed to New Ways for Families: Parent-Child Counseling.

Date____________ Licensed Mental Health Professional __________________

© 2010 High Conflict Institute, LLC **www.NewWays4Families.com**

Client Name ______________________________

Case Number______________________________

VERIFICATION OF COMPLETION OF NEW WAYS FOR FAMILIES: PARENT-CHILD COUNSELING

Date first contacted by parent _____

Date Received Parent's Behavioral Declaration _____

Date Received copy of court orders from parent _____

Date Received Parent's Reply Declaration _____

Date Parent attended 1st Individual Session _____

Upon completion, the Parent-Child Counselor should copy this sheet, sign it and submit it to the client. The client may provide it to anyone he or she chooses, including other professionals and/or the court.

I hereby verify that _____ has attended at least 3 sessions of Step 3 of New Ways for Families: Parent-Child Counseling of 60-90 minutes each with his or her child/ren . I hereby verify that he or she has completed all of the corresponding written assignments for 3 sessions of New Ways Parent-Child Counseling.

I believe it would be appropriate/inappropriate (circle one) for _____ _____ to proceed to Step 4 of New Ways for Families: Family (or Court) Decision-Making.

Date_____ Licensed Mental Health Professional _____

© 2010 High Conflict Institute, LLC   **www.NewWays4Families.com**

Client Name _____

Case Number _____

CPSIA information can be obtained at www.ICGtesting.com
Printed in the USA
LVOW13s0230111013

356477LV00005B/87/P